Eva Melusine Thieme

KILIMANJARO DIARIES

Or, How I Spent a Week Dreaming of
Toilets, Drinking Crappy Water, and
Making Bad Jokes While Having the Time
of My Life

ISBN-13: 978-1497599383
ISBN-10: 1497599385

www.evamelusinethieme.com

Cover Art and Design: Nicole El Salamoni
Editor: Julie van Pelt
Copy Editor: Ros Brodie

To my mother
who taught me the love of books
and who would have loved
to read this one.

CONTENTS

Kilimanjaro Diaries

PROLOGUE

<u>September 2009</u>

It's a cold and windy day in Overland Park, Kansas. I'm sitting at my computer, not sure what to think.

Do we stay where we are, or do we move our family of six to Johannesburg, South Africa? It would be yet another continent to add to our list of places to call home. It would be exciting. And it would give the kids an opportunity to go to school in a new country, something they haven't experienced yet.

In addition, it would allow me to upgrade my job description to "expat wife" – an idea that seems vastly more alluring than my daily housewife drudgery of cooking, overseeing homework, and splitting up sibling squabbles.

But we've only been in Kansas for three years, after a period of frequent moves all over the country, and aren't particularly stir-crazy. The kids are happy in their various schools, I've got the sports scene figured out, we have an orthodontist and a hairdresser we like – in short, our life is one big, comfortable routine.

What's more, I've just shut the lid of my laptop in disgust. I was looking at some web pages in an effort to find out more about life in South Africa, and I'm utterly discouraged by what I've seen. If I am to believe what is posted in one expat forum after another, South Africa – and the city of Johannesburg in particular – is a cesspit of crime. If we are so foolish as to move there, I have read, we'll be carjacked and possibly murdered before we even make it from the airport to our house. We'll have fingers chopped off to get to our jewelry, we'll be accosted by gun-wielding thugs when we retrieve money from an ATM, and we'll have rocks thrown into our windshields when waiting at a red light while criminals make off with our cell-phones. If we survive all of this, we'll probably die in a car wreck because everyone is advised to "never stop at a red light."

Wouldn't it be irresponsible to move to such a dangerous place? It sure seems like it. All of our friends and relatives apparently agree. "Johannesburg? You must be out of your mind," is one of the milder reactions we've gotten when cautiously floating the idea in recent weeks. Just going there by ourselves, is the consensus, would be foolish enough. But taking our children to the world's murder capital, a label that the city of Johannesburg – unfairly or not – has been stuck with since the downfall of the apartheid regime, is tantamount to gross negligence, if not worse. "Don't go," we're hearing from all sides.

Perhaps it's because I hate being told what I can't do. Or perhaps a life of moves, first without children and then with them, has programmed my inner clock to once again become impatient for a change of scenery, routines be damned. What if there is another side to life in Africa, one that I'll have to dig deeper to understand?

I'm struck by a sudden thought, and I open my computer once again. As expected, Googling "Kilimanjaro" yields an entirely more promising collection of links than "Expat in Johannesburg," and before long I'm completely hooked.

A seed has been planted.

PART I – THE PLANNING

"Nowadays, when all the world is on the move, and all sorts of traveling requisites are at the traveler's command, the difficulty is not so much to know what to take as what to omit."

– Dr. Hans Meyer, first to summit Mount Kilimanjaro

To Climb or Not to Climb Kilimanjaro

December 2011

We did move to South Africa in early 2010, arriving quite safely at our house that first day, fingers and windshields intact. Without waiting for a new routine to settle into, we embarked on a whirlwind of travel and adventure, fueled in equal measure by the knowledge that any expat assignment eventually ends and must be exploited as well as the breathtaking beauty of our surroundings. By now almost two years have passed, and the snows of Kilimanjaro are looming as distant as ever, even though I've been harboring the secret idea of climbing to Africa's roof from the moment I stepped onto its shores.

I can't tell you what drove me to read up on the ins and outs of climbing Kilimanjaro before we even settled on a South African school to send our children to. I'm not a mountain climber. I'm not particularly outdoorsy. I don't even like going for walks all that much and would rather sit at my computer with a steaming cup of coffee. Klaus, my husband, often raves about the "fresh air" in an attempt to lure me and the kids – who are often as firmly glued to their electronic devices as I am to mine – out into the great outdoors. But you know what? I vastly prefer warm air over fresh air.

I'm rather a couch potato, if I'm completely honest. I do like the odd adventure, but mainly for the purpose of writing about it afterwards. While I'm living it, I usually can't wait to get it behind me already so that I can take my shower and start my story, which invariably is funnier in hindsight than while it's happening.

I'm not one to make bucket lists, either. I do like to make lists, but they are of the mundane variety: "Make dentist appointment," "Repair sprinkler head," and, lately, "Figure out how the hell to kill the mole that's destroying our lawn." If I did make any bucket lists, climbing a mountain is possibly the last thing I'd put on there. I'm terrified of heights, and I might even be more terrified of being cold, both of which are hard to avoid when you go mountain-climbing.

In fact, I can come up with a million other reasons why *not* to climb Kilimanjaro. I might get sick, for instance. I'm not a hypochondriac, but the ways you could possibly get sick on Mount Kilimanjaro, a little bit of research will tell you, are mind-boggling. Apart from the dreaded altitude sickness forcing many a traveler to a premature descent (or killing those who don't have the good sense to turn around), there are a myriad of other illnesses that could make life miserable for you on the mountain. If you don't get attacked by a vicious stomach ailment from contaminated water, get an infected blister on your heel, or suffer from a broken bone after tumbling down a deep scree slope, you might still succumb to illness after your trip when malaria – only a threat during the two nights at the base hotel but that might be all it takes – catches up with you when you think you're safely home again.

I'm also not really looking for any more excitement in my life. From that fateful day we decided to ignore all the warnings and give South Africa a try, we've embraced expat life and made it our mission to take in as much of the country as possible while we have the chance. It's so easy to get sucked in by the demands of everyday life, wherever you might live, and totally forget that you are in the most exotic place you've ever been. We know this from experience. South Africa isn't the first expat assignment for our family, you see. When the boys were little, at the end of the last century (I love being able to say that!), we lived in Singapore for a few years. Incidentally, this was also the beginning of my housewife existence, as it was Klaus' job that took us there, not mine. As soon as we arrived I took on my new role with a vengeance and with as much drive as I had previously mustered for marketing plans and team-building exercises. I got so busy instituting nap regimens, sticker charts, and potty-training routines, let alone trying to convince reluctant contractors ("Speak no English-lah") to fix our air conditioning, that I almost forgot there was a tantalizing and exotic world out there to be explored. We did venture to some normally faraway places like New Zealand and Indonesia, but in retrospect not nearly enough of them. We departed, pregnant with our third child and full of regrets about countries not visited.

So far we've more than made up for it here, exploring not only South Africa, which already offers a lifetime of interesting vacation spots, but also even more exotic locales such as Victoria Falls, Mozambique, Mauritius, Namibia, and Zanzibar. We've been kissed by elephants, petted a cheetah, dived with great white sharks, held a newborn lion, hurled ourselves off bridges and out of airplanes (okay, not all of us), swum in the Okavango, and paddled down the Zambezi. We've gotten as much adventure out of this life as one possibly can.

Surely I, a housewife and mother of four children with more than enough on my plate, do not need to go scale one of the major mountains in the world?

And yet, that is precisely what I want to do. My gut tells me that if I leave Africa without at least trying to see the summit of Mount Kilimanjaro, I'll feel incomplete.

And it's not because of some yearning to add another exotic destination to the list. All I can think is that deep within me I must have a longing to do something meaningful, something to break up the years between child-bearing and retirement, to scale something of magnitude. But not too much magnitude, mind you, and if you think about it, Mount Kilimanjaro is the perfect candidate for just such a mid-magnitude type of endeavor.

It's high – high enough to make for some labored breathing up top, if you even make it that far – but not prohibitively high. It's the highest mountain on an entire continent and the highest free-standing mountain in the world, rendering your feat just a little bit more special. And consider the latitude. If I am to have any chance of not freezing to death on a mountain's summit, the only one in the world sitting smack on the equator is the obvious choice.

Or maybe Ernest Hemingway is to blame, although I've never been a big fan of his writing. Who doesn't equate "The Snows of Kilimanjaro" with sweeping African savannah, camps in the bush, and servants aplenty to obey your every command and guide you on the right path while carrying your gun?

I admit it's this last image that sealed the deal for me: the prospect of someone else lugging not my gun but my sleeping bag and wet wipes and water bottles together with tents and a mountain of food for seven days while I leisurely stroll behind.

Okay, not so leisurely, it turns out. But you get the picture.

Where else but Africa can you expect to be completely pampered when embarking on a week of hardship?

It's late 2011 and I've decided that if I am to climb Mount Kilimanjaro, or Kili, as it is fondly called among insiders, it's now or never. We don't know how much longer we'll get to stay. Expat assignments come and go, and ours has gone on for almost two years. Of course you can undertake a Kili climb from anywhere in the world, but Johannesburg, while we still live here, is the perfect starting point for this quest. You get a bit of a leg up in terms of altitude, because you'll be starting from 1,600 meters instead of sea level, you save yourself the flight from overseas, and I'm also sure we can probably book cheaper packages locally than if we lived abroad.

I broach the subject with a group of friends, and in the typical South African fashion I've so come to love, what was only a vague idea at the beginning becomes reality over two bottles of Chardonnay.

"Let's do it," pronounces our friend Mike when he and his wife Jacky and Klaus and I are having dinner at their house. And just like that, a plan is hatched. A few more friends are brought into the fold, some research is done over the ensuing weeks, a tour organizer found, and a group trip booked. I can honestly say that other than replying to a few emails, I don't have a hand in any of this. It's good to have friends who'll plan a trip for you.

Of course it's not quite as simple as that. As Mike will tell you, it did take quite a bit of planning on his part. What originally started it all, in a fortunate confluence of events for the rest of us, was his son Dylan, age 16, telling him one day last year that he wanted to climb Kili as a father-son adventure.

"Where did this idea suddenly come from?" asked Mike.

"Well, it's just that you're getting old," was the unflattering reply. "I want to climb Kili with you while you're not *too* old."

He didn't have to be told twice. Even though I'm sure he'll still be sauntering up mountains well into his eighties, Mike decided that this was the year for his third Kilimanjaro climb, before Dylan left for university. And it just so happened that I was mulling it over in my head at around the same time. I had been trying to find a way to convince our oldest son Max, also 16, to come along, and the idea of one or more of his friends going on the trip was welcome news. It would make the task of selling a week of walking on foot far from an Internet connection that much easier. I may also have promised a container full of homemade cookie dough.

When I say that some research was done and a trip was booked, I'm not being quite honest. There was also a succession of what Mike likes to call "pub meetings" to presumably talk about the details of the trip, but in reality to consume a good many more bottles of wine to seal the deal. Whatever the actual climb will bring, I already have fond memories of the first part of our adventure – these long evenings of sitting at the bar in Mike and Jacky's house for hours, trading jokes and battle stories from earlier trips.

I've achieved clarity about one other aspect. When I originally shared my dream with Klaus, he sounded pleased, if not overly excited, with the idea of a Kili climb. Like me, he thought it would be a great bonding experience for Max and us. Max, being the first-born (and, by extension, the first to become a teenager) has to bear the brunt of what I admit are often learn-as-you-go parenting practices, and as of the last three years our relationship with him has had more than one rocky patch. Spending time with him one on one, away from home, and away from the magical pull of electronic devices, might be a good way to renew our bonds. Our three other kids are too young, or too prone to altitude sickness, or too prone, in some cases, to incessant whining when confronted with the slightest incline to be conquered on foot. But Max, we thought, was cut out to accompany us, even if he'd probably need a lot of convincing.

Then one day Klaus and I took a hike – I'd rather call it a stroll – around Franschhoek Pass in the Eastern Cape, and he soon started grumbling.

"This path is too uneven," he complained. "I can't see any of the countryside when I always have to keep my eyes down."

"Really?" I called back from ahead. I had just been thinking the opposite. That this was the kind of walk I enjoyed. It was a challenge.

When we shared stories about our childhoods while carefully stepping over boulders on our way uphill, it emerged that Klaus used to love his family's Sunday strolls on wide paved Northern German roads, flat as a pancake, while breathing in the fresh air. Germans call this a *Spaziergang*. When I was child, I hated a *Spaziergang*. I hated it with a passion, even if it only lasted an hour, leading me to whine about it without end. (Don't tell my children I said that.) But if you gave me a day-long hike in the Swiss Alps, clambering up grueling slopes, crossing a glacier, stopping at a sparkling stream where dams could be built, I was in heaven and never complained. Or, as my brothers might correct me, at least I complained less. The point is that I love a good challenge, while I hate walking just for the sake of walking. I mean, if there is a paved road, why not ride a bicycle to get there faster?

Klaus, on the other hand, didn't like the ruggedness of our half-hour hike, and this made him realize that he would like seven whole days of it even less. So it was decided right then and there that if I wanted to climb Kilimanjaro, I'd have to do it without him. It was Max I had been worried about, but it turned out my husband was the one I couldn't convince. Even Mike's persistent prodding over the course of our pub evenings has not been enticing enough to sway him.

Now that the plans have been made, I'm a bit uncomfortable with the idea of going on this adventure without Klaus. Not that I'm one of those wives who don't dare undertake anything without their husbands. I've taken the kids on plenty of trips Klaus couldn't join us on, including thousands of miles on the road, and it has never bothered me to be the sole adult. Sure, I would have enjoyed his company, but I am perfectly fine loading and unloading a car on my own or navigating an airport terminal.

It's the same this time around; easier, in fact, because I won't be outnumbered by my children. Nevertheless, I'm still uneasy. On those previous occasions when he didn't accompany us, there were perfectly good reasons for it. They were necessitated by circumstance, were agreed upon by mutual consent. We'd look at our schedules together, figure out the best itinerary, and Klaus would book the flights. I hate booking flights. If it was up to me to book the flights, we might never go anywhere.

But this is the first time, I realize, that I want to go on a trip badly enough to make my own travel arrangements. Or, as it happens, find someone else to make the arrangements. It's just me, between the two of us, who wants to climb Mount Kilimanjaro, and I'm prepared to leave him behind. It feels a little bit like I'm choosing the mountain over the husband. We've been married for almost 20 years and in all this time we have made all decisions jointly, have wanted the same things, and have more or less shared the same tastes. Even though he is very supportive of my decision, I still can't help feeling that I'm abandoning him in some small way in my quest for personal fulfillment.

I do think that Max will want to come, or at least I hope so. He has been evasive on the subject so far, having learned that telling me "maybe" and "I'm not so sure" goes over much better than an outright "no, there is no way in hell," his more typical reaction as a kid who'd rather not challenge himself to try out something new and unproven.

Especially if he can't be one hundred percent sure that he will master it on the first try. I have some perfectionist tendencies, and I see them a thousand times reflected in Max. It can be quite comical watching him bake a cake, for instance, measuring and squinting and sifting minute quantities of ingredients to make sure they are precisely in the amounts prescribed, not one gram more or less.

And, like most perfectionists, he'd rather not do something at all than risk potential failure.

It will also pain him to leave the beloved Xbox behind for over a week, as well as the comforts of our house and his daily routine. But, like me, he likes a good challenge. He once raced me up the stairwell to the 21st floor of a hotel in Manhattan, losing me after three flights and greeting me nonchalantly with a big smile when I finally dragged myself into the room, tongue hanging to the floor and babbling incoherently.

It will be a great experience conquering Mount Kilimanjaro together. I just hope he won't race me up the mountain.

A Pair of New Boots…
And a Countdown

February 2012, seven months to go

I've done it. I've bought my hiking boots for Kilimanjaro.

The boots are all I have so far, but nevertheless it feels different now. It feels like I'm in. Let the countdown begin! I have seven months in which to get my act together and gather all the needed supplies, minus the boots.

We picked September for our climb, for several reasons. It falls into the South African school holidays, for one. Not that taking Max and the other two boys who are coming with us out of school for ten days would pose a major obstacle. This is Africa, after all, and I reckon a school that is not too fussy about children walking barefoot (though always in uniforms) to their classes will grant some leeway when it comes to skipping them altogether, especially in pursuit of such a life-changing endeavor.

There was also the matter of coordinating ten people's schedules and agreeing on one date. It's a small miracle we've been able to settle on a date less than ten years from now.

But mainly, we picked September because of the climate on Mount Kilimanjaro. Let me tell you, researching the weather and finding out which time of year is best for a climb is not as easily done as it might seem. I assume that tour operators have to weigh success rates against the desire to be booked year-round, and so depending on which opinion you read, you will find a lot of pros and cons for a variety of months.

Basically, there are two rainy seasons on the mountain, one shorter one and one longer one. You want to avoid getting into those. Except everyone else does the same, so the better the weather, the bigger the crowds.

The driest months are August, September, and October, with August being colder and October, while warmer, becoming increasingly cloudy. Of the three, September seems to be the Goldilocks choice – moderate temperatures and clear skies.

The other dry season is January through mid-March, also a good (and popular) time of year for Kili climbs. It's warmer than in September, but the chance of precipitation is also slightly higher. Traffic at both times is high. If you want to avoid the crowds, the best time of year is probably early March, but you run the increasing risk of getting into the rainy season spanning late March through June.

June sounds like the worst time of year to me – cold and wet. Only July might be even worse, because it's still cold and only slightly less wet, but the traffic is also high, probably due to the European vacation schedule. Imagine huge crowds slipping and sliding through rivers of mud, and you won't want to pick July.

November through December is the other rainy season and I can't find any good reason for picking those months either, unless of course you get it into your mind that you absolutely have to ring in the New Year from the top of Africa.

My head was spinning the first time I sifted through this sea of information. It became a lot clearer once I grouped it into categories:

January – March: One of the peak seasons on Kilimanjaro, warm temperatures, a fairly low chance of rain (except toward the end of March), good visibility, high traffic (but less so than in September).

April – June: Main rainy season, with decreasing temperatures toward June, avoided by most climbers and even a few tour operators.

July: Decreasing rainfall, nights still very cold, increasing crowds.

August – October: Peak season on Kili, driest months of the year, good visibility, increasing temperatures, increasing cloud cover toward the end of October, very high traffic (especially in September).

November – December: Rainy season, low traffic but crowds returning over Christmas.

There's also a lot of contradictory information out there, especially when it comes to temperature. Is it June that's the coldest month, or September? Or perhaps even January? Common sense seems to dictate that no matter the average temperature, rain must be avoided. I for one do not like getting wet. This means that late August to mid-October, or January and February, are the most auspicious dates for a successful Kili climb.

We've picked September. So has everyone else, I think.

There is still plenty of time until September and no reason to fret yet, other than a nagging feeling of needing to start a new blog counting down the days. Everybody attempting a Kili ascent seems to have a blog for it. Since I already have a blog chronicling our expat life in South Africa, I create a new category called "Kili Climb" and lay out my intentions in the first post I write. I get a lot of encouragement from my readers, coupled with the absolute certainty that now that I've outed myself in this way, there is no turning back.

In addition to their blog, everyone attempting a Kili ascent seems to have created a charity drive to dedicate the climb to. But I cannot think of a single noble cause in the name of which I might adequately subject myself to this hardship. The only charity case that comes to mind is that of me having to somehow come up with the money to fund this rather expensive venture. I'm afraid my hike will have to remain noble-cause-less and, frankly, rather selfish. I mean, a week without cooking for a family of six – where's the self-sacrifice in that?

There are two reasons I've bought the hiking boots now rather than later: 1) They were on sale, and this being South Africa, where shoes of any kind are inordinately expensive, shoe sales demand your immediate attention; and 2) They should be broken in before the trip, because the last thing you want on the mountain is a blister on your foot.

I have grand plans to lace up these boots every morning and walk to school with the kids (and perhaps even carry their bags). Except I've now had them for an entire week and they've been sitting in the closet. The kids have been walking to school by themselves, like they always do.

That's precisely why I bought the boots so early: so that I could have plenty of time to procrastinate. From what I've read and been told by Kili veterans, taking daily or at least weekly walks, with or without your boots on, is the best preparation for a Kili climb. Forget running as if you're preparing for a marathon – that's not the kind of fitness that's needed. This comes as welcome news to me, because I hate running.

Not only is it apparently not needed, it may even be counterproductive. There are plenty of stories where trained athletes have been forced off the mountain by altitude sickness or other ailments. Martina Navratilova comes to mind. I've been browsing through other people's

Kilimanjaro stories, and hers, from about a year ago, reads like a regular drama: intestinal cramps, heavy rains, altitude sickness, a rescue down the mountain at night, a hospital stay to recover from pulmonary edema – all this while being accompanied up the mountain by her very own team doctor.

I can't foresee what drama our trip will bring, but I know for a fact that there won't be any team doctors on *our* mountain.

I should also tell you that I am, in fact, participating in a boot camp. Once, sometimes twice a week, I drag myself to the cricket field at the kids' school and let myself be ordered around for an hour by a drill sergeant armed with a stopwatch. She is not unlike Martina Navratilova, come to think of it, though better looking. She makes us do all sorts of cruel exercises, including several kilometers of running, which I told you I hate, and she generally whips us into shape, one agonizing burpee at a time. (If you've done a boot camp yourself, you will know exactly what a burpee is, as one never forgets them; if you haven't done a boot camp yet, you may not want to know.)

But I don't think the boot camp will be essential for a successful Kili climb. It's just something I happen to be engaged in while passing time before the climb starts. I'm not even sure why I'm doing it, but my friend Monia, who is climbing Kili with us, talked me into it. I should also mention that Monia has successfully climbed Kili before. She is one of those crazy people who are doing it a second time. If she is doing a boot camp, maybe it's not a bad idea to follow her lead.

I've also bought a daypack. I doubt that the daypack needs breaking in. But I've already bought it anyway, because I so love the idea of the daypack. Like I said before, if I am to strike "scale a mountain" off my bucket list, even though I don't have a bucket list, it will be so much more convenient if the mountain in question is one where all I have to carry is a little daypack for my jacket, a water bottle, and a camera. For the rest we were told to pack a duffel bag for the porters to carry on their heads.

I cannot wait to take a picture of the porters carrying our bags on their heads, because I'm still working on an "Africans carrying stuff on their heads" photo collage for my blog. Although they will probably be way ahead of me jogging up the mountain, and I will never even see them.

By the way, in case you're wondering: I've put on the hiking boots. If I start this early, I'm sure there is a teensy chance they'll be broken in, even though all I've been doing so far is sitting at the computer and typing this diary.

The Shopping List

It's a good thing our climb is still six months away, because my Kili supply stash is pitiful. And it's not for lack of trying.

I've been in and out of the outdoor store Trappers about a dozen times. It's well stocked and, even better, it's next to a Pick'n Pay grocery store, allowing for quick reconnaissance forays while I'm in the vicinity. The Trappers sales clerk, Julie, knows me by name. She has patiently outlined all the options and shown me more or less everything they have in stock.

But maybe therein lies the problem: I am completely overwhelmed. Every time I think I've zeroed in on a sleeping bag, for instance, I feel the strong need to conduct more online research, read customer reviews, and find out what other deals can be had. I've been known to spend hours settling on a brand of suntan lotion, so purchasing something as expensive as a sleeping bag is not a matter I'll decide on a whim.

I also get terribly distracted by all the colorful displays around me stacked high with unnecessary stuff. Or perhaps not so unnecessary. Who is to say a microfiber towel won't be the very thing I'll most long for on Kilimanjaro? It practically weighs nothing, and it is oh so soft! But what size to get? And more importantly, which color? How about the complete plate and cutlery set, neatly nestled, made from hard anodized aluminum and in its very own drawstring bag? Or should I go for the more expensive top-of-the-line titanium version, complete with a spork (spoon+fork=spork, my kids had to teach me that) praised for its indestructability?

Julie, to her immense credit, has pushed none of this on me. Rather, she saves me from the eating utensils I've already put in my basket, together with the stormproof lighting system (withstands gale-force winds), by gently pointing out that all our food will be cooked and served for us on Kilimanjaro. Almost regretfully, I place the spork and plates back on the shelf and resist tantalizing flashlights, carbine hooks, an "ultimate survival kit," and a satin-finish knife and multi-tool as I make my way to the cash register.

Perhaps I should take the advice of none other than the man who stood on Kilimanjaro's summit for the very first time in history over 120 years ago: "Nowadays, when all the world is on the move, and all sorts of traveling requisites are at the traveler's command, the difficulty is not so much to know what to take as what to omit, and beginners are far more likely to err in taking too much than in taking too little."

These words were written by Dr. Hans Meyer, Germany's very own Sir Edmund Hillary, the first to successfully scale Kilimanjaro in 1889. He specifically counsels against bringing along collapsible tent furniture, lamps and lanterns, and "the India rubber air beds and pillows of the advertisements." If there had been carbine hooks and sporks and satin-finish knives in his day, he would have added them to his "don't be tempted" list, I'm sure of it.

I can't help but feel a certain kinship with Hans Meyer. After all, he is a fellow German. Klaus and I, having met at university and completing our studies together as well as moving into the corporate world in lock-step, decided to leave our native Germany in our early twenties to pursue business degrees, and by extension hopefully a future life, in the United States. Our plan worked. We settled in North Carolina, got married, and started a family, making Raleigh our new home base before setting out on our more recent forays as expats. We became American citizens somewhere along the way, but we are still loyal to our German roots (particularly, when Germany competes in the soccer world cup).

But what most makes me feel as if Hans Meyer is a long-lost friend is not his German origin but his way to put into words exactly what I'm thinking. Even though he lived so long before me, he seems to have felt exactly the same about his shopping expeditions as I do now, in the year 2012. My shopping successes so far can very safely be listed in the "too little" column – at this rate I'm in no danger of taking too much – and the fact that this father of all Kili climbers seems to give his nod of approval makes me feel much better.

Soon enough, however, I feel as though I need to expand my supply list beyond the boots and daypack, and so I decide to make another excursion to Trappers, long list of recommended Kili supplies in hand. I don't particularly like shopping (let's pause briefly to hear loud protestations from Klaus about where the hell then all our money is going), and I'm also a bit of a perfectionist, which is not a good combination.

I look around in the store and see a Columbia jacket that might be useful. While I do own a perfectly fine ski jacket, it's unfortunately stowed away somewhere in the depths of a Kansas self-storage, along with a few pieces of furniture we decided to leave behind. (Note to future expats: always take all your cold-weather gear with you; you never know if you might suddenly get the urge to climb one of the world's Seven Peaks.)

I try on the jacket, and it is nice. No, it is spectacular! It is also very expensive. It has something like 20 zippered pockets and 30 layers and comes with a virtual guarantee that it will keep me warm, once I put all my limbs in the correct crevices and properly shutter all the closures. It's a high-tech piece of equipment, no doubt, and will probably require its own training regimen in preparation for the climb.

Then I start looking at pants to go with the jacket. Do you know what drives me crazy in the world of outdoor gear shopping? Nothing matches! I try out a succession of different non-matching combinations, all while a silent debate is raging within my head that it won't matter one teensy bit by the end of Day One what color pants I've got tucked in my bag. And still I can't bring myself to give any of them the green light.

Because I'm determined to leave the store with at least one purchase in the proverbial bag, I think back to Hans Meyer's counsel. "The dearest proves the cheapest in the end" is another pearl of wisdom I recall from his book, and I know with sudden clarity that the sleeping bag, in addition to the boots, is where I need to splurge. I throw all my online research and shipping-it-from-the-United-States schemes to the wind and select the most expensive down sleeping bag with the lowest possible temperature rating and take it to the cash register, cost be damned.

I instantly feel better. The sleeping bag is a huge item to check off. I'll have to return for another one for Max once they get more supplies in, but now that I know which one I want, it'll be easily done.

There is one last thing I decide to get today: socks! When I bought the boots last month, I was handed a random pair of socks to test the right fit, and I now remember that they were absolutely amazing. I didn't want to take them off again, ever. It is that particular brand of socks I *have* to have two pairs of, and it's easy to spot them on the shelf: one has a huge "L" on it for left, the other an "R." Perhaps it's such sophisticated markings as much as the comfort that urges me to make these, and none other, my intimate traveling companions, even though they're the most expensive socks I'll ever own. Something tells me I'm going to need all the help I can get to make it up that mountain. If it comes in the form of fancy socks, that's the least I can invest in.

I feel rather pleased with my success today, and when I get home I start a small pile with what I have: boots, socks, daypack, and sleeping bag – four items. Eight, if I count each of the boots and socks. That's one way to make my list look a fraction more substantial. But I have the nagging feeling that everyone else in our group is way ahead of me in the packing department.

What's worse, I have to get everything in two sets – one for me and one for Max. Dragging him to go shoe shopping will be another chore in its own right. At least I *did* like shopping when I was a teenager, even if it's a bother for me now, but getting Max into a store is like herding an elephant. It'll be a miracle if I can keep him in there long enough to try on at least one pair of boots, and it had better be the one that fits, because he'll refuse to put on another.

As I stand there surveying my stash, I am struck by a sudden thought. I run all the way downstairs into the garage, and there it is, pushed way onto the back of a shelf between the paper towels and the soccer cleats: a carton full of "Little Hotties – up to 8 hours of pure heat."

Klaus bought this box of hand warmers at Costco during our last Kansas winter. We were never going to use them all, but if my weakness is indecision in the face of too many choices, his is an irrational fondness for mass discount stores. Along with my ski jacket, this box was meant to be stored somewhere in Kansas instead of being dragged halfway around the world. It was designated to go to storage, not in the container, for who needs hand warmers in Africa? But now I'm very happy to have it. You might recall that there are two things I fear most in life that mountain climbing is bound to threaten me with, and my hand warmers will help me conquer one of them. They will be the one item in my duffel bag not mentioned on any official Kili websites.

I'll probably bring the entire box.

Just for good measure, I sit down and type my very own Kilimanjaro packing list, cobbled together from conversations with previous hikers, Julie's professional input (she is herself a Kili veteran), the ever-practical Hans Meyer himself ("woolen socks and lacing boots that come up well over the ankle!"), my very own additions (inflatable pillow and hand warmers), and many a time-sucking foray into the depths of various travel websites. Klaus accuses me of researching everything I shop for to death, and quite possibly he is right on that point. The shopping list is the one area of Kili preparations I've taken quite seriously.

When I'm done with the list, I instantly feel better and one big step closer to Uhuru Peak. There is nothing like a good list to make you feel as if you've accomplished something of magnitude.

A Garden Trowel? Seriously?

April 2012, five months to go

"(1) Garden trowel or small shovel (ablutions)."

Somehow I previously missed this item (optional) on my Kili packing list, but now it is glaring me in the face. Sometimes it takes a clear visual of things to come to get you thinking. I have not thought about the toilet situation on Mount Kilimanjaro, I admit. But the garden trowel, together with *(2) Rolls of toilet paper,* has me now thinking of nothing else.

It's not that I'm easily disgusted. I'm a mother of four and have had my fair share of revolting situations to deal with. As I've mentioned, I'm also not American by birth, which based on my not-so-scientific research seems to equip me with a higher degree of resiliency against stuff that might gross others out.

I will never forget the time I was bent over a toilet tank with a co-worker at my first job out of graduate school, trying to figure out why it wasn't refilling. She had asked me, the more senior of the two of us by a few weeks, to come help, because in our small start-up company there wasn't anyone else to call. So I did the only thing one can do in that situation, which is to reach into the tank and untangle that flimsy little chain so that the flap can close over the drain.

My co-worker recoiled in horror. "Did you just reach into the toilet with your bare hands?" she asked, incredulous.

"Not the toilet. The tank. And the water is the same as what's coming out of the tap."

But nothing I said could convince her that my hands hadn't been contaminated in some horrible way, and for weeks afterwards I sensed she was giving me a wider berth than necessary every time we saw each other.

I'm also not overly modest. Not living an American childhood gives you a leg up in that regard as well. Germans not only don't care much if anyone glimpses their naked butt when changing at a public swimming pool, some of them practically seem to go out of their way to showcase their nether regions, like the old men jogging on Baltic Sea beaches bundled in thick woolen sweaters (the weather on Baltic Sea beaches is almost never balmy) but no other clothing at all. I did draw the line once, when a German doctor giving me a physical told me to undress (you'll find nary a gown in any German doctor's office) and then proceeded not with the expected examination but with a vision test. Or, rather, I *wanted* to draw the line, but standing right in front of him stark naked reciting the alphabet seemed the most expedient way to get it over with. I do not particularly cherish that memory, but for the most part I'm not obsessive about privacy.

Why then has the image of the garden trowel lodged itself so indelibly in my brain? I think it's as simple as this: I can't *go* when someone might be watching. I just can't. We had to stop by the roadside many times on a recent road trip through Namibia, for lack of encountering any human habitation for miles and miles, and unlike the male members of our family I could never relieve myself on those occasions. Even that day we improbably had three tire punctures in the space of a few hours, without a soul coming to our rescue, I could not bring myself to squat down in the barren landscape with nothing but vast stretches of open vista in every direction.

This is why finding the perfect location for ablutions on Mount Kilimanjaro, with or without the garden trowel, will require some work.

I can't help mentioning the garden trowel to Max, who also hasn't thought of the toilet situation until now, and it clearly is a mistake. He looks at me with panic in his eyes. I want to say more, but he cuts me off.

"Stop it right there," he says. "Not one more word!"

There is no one in our family more meticulous about washing hands than Max, and the mere thought of not having his very own private toilet, let alone any toilet at all, is enough to make him want to drop out before the climb has even begun.

As much as the garden trowel sounds disturbing (where do you stow it after the feat?), the alternative might be worse. Most of the camps along the various Kili routes are outfitted with "long drop toilets," and I have yet to find an online resource that has anything good to say about them. "The facilities here were described as 'long-drop toilets', though it was memorably apparent that at this stage the drop was not nearly as long as it had been," is the most concise and at the same time vivid description of these toilets I've been able to find, stemming from the not-so-reassuringly named article "Kilimanjaro? Well it nearly killed me" in *The Guardian* by Tim Moore.

Not that I needed anyone to tell me that. I know all about drop toilets, and they scare the living shit out of me – sorry, I couldn't resist.

My perhaps irrational fear of drop toilets dates back to when I was around 12 years old. Out of the blue, my parents had decided to buy an old castle. If this sounds somewhat strange, keep in mind that I grew up in Europe, and they've got castles practically growing out of their ears over there. "Um, what should we get Mary for her

40th birthday? Oh, let's just buy her an old castle." Or perhaps: "Want to come to Paris with us for the weekend? Sorry I can't, I've got plans to go castle shopping."

Even so, your parents buying on old castle was definitely not cool, especially when it was revealed to me that from now on we'd be spending our summers renovating our castle in some godforsaken southern German village rather than sauntering along sunny Italian and Spanish beaches as in years past.

Still, being rather a tomboy, I had images of Ivanhoe and Robin Hood dancing in my head when we pulled into the courtyard that first summer. But what I saw was more a large and rather plain farmhouse than anything close to what the word "castle" might evoke. Instead of turrets and princesses, there was a crumbling wall overgrown with weeds and a stable full of milk cows. The farmer who lived there had neglected it over the years (if not centuries, judging from his shriveled face), and was only selling it now to finance construction of a new house on the lot next door, no doubt threatened into this course of action by a mutiny at the hands of the women in his life.

Because, by golly, that house was old! Something like 600 years. And from what I could tell, the bathroom facilities hadn't been updated much since the late 1500s. There was one single dark bathroom with peeling wallpaper featuring a few 20th century additions like a cracked tub and a moldy plastic curtain, but the first summer we vacationed there we had to share the house with the farmer and his family. My choices were using the nominally modern amenities of this bathroom at the terrifying risk of coming across the wizened farmer and his equally wizened wife in a state of undress, or using the ancient drop toilet dating from the castle's beginnings in the 14th century which we had all to ourselves in the part of the house we were sequestered in.

I chose the solitude of the drop toilet. To get there, you had to walk up a creaky staircase illuminated by a single light bulb. Then you had to shimmy open the door and turn one of those large iron keys – you know, the ones they present to important people when giving out the key to the city – with all the power you could muster to lock the door behind you. You felt for, more than glimpsed, the wooden platform in the dim light, then you lifted the lid and set it somewhere next to you, all the while trying hard not to breathe too deeply. But however valiantly you avoided air passing through your nose passages, you couldn't escape eventually inhaling the most awful stink, made worse by the fact that physics somehow seems to dictate that a cold and smelly draft of air always seems to blow up and right onto your ass when you are perched on a drop toilet.

The one thing that could be said for that particular one was that there was no risk of splashing. Living up to its name, there was definitely a drop – two stories' worth of drop to be exact – so that the muted sound of matter making contact only reached your ears after a reassuring delay. Still, to my young teenage self, the idea that below me lay the accumulation of possibly several generations' worth of excrement was enough to almost make me faint.

Somehow I survived that summer and the terror of what I now think might well have been the very last German *Plumpsklo* in existence. (*Plumps* is best translated as *thud*; there you have it, a "thud toilet," in case you needed a more graphic description.) But maybe you'll now understand why the phrase *Kili drop toilets* has stoked such fear in me.

The good news is that we have five more months to contemplate the use of a garden trowel for our ablutions. In fact, there is a whole lot else to contemplate in those five months, and even though I tend not to worry too much about the future, I am beginning to appreciate what a monstrous task we have set ourselves.

I'm not just talking about the hard work of scaling 5,895 meters (19,340 feet) in seven days. Walking seven to eight hours every day, sometimes even longer. Sleeping on a thin mat, because anything thicker would be too heavy (15 kilograms allowed). Making do without a shower. Having blisters on my feet. Battling with altitude sickness (50 percent of hikers never make it to the top). Being extremely hot, and being extremely cold.

I'm not saying those aren't valid concerns, but the ones I'm talking about are of a slightly different nature. Like, how can I possibly survive without a cappuccino for a whole week? Or without my Kindle with its daily dose of *The New York Times*? I don't suppose there will be an Internet connection up there. But just on the odd chance, I might tote my Kindle up anyway. On a recent trip to a rather remote area of South Africa I hiked to the top of a nearby hill every morning just so that I could download that day's newspaper. I briefly imagine myself standing on the roof of Africa, waving my Kindle in this direction and that while everyone else is busy hoisting flags and taking pictures.

I suppose I'll be happy without email for a week, but I won't be happy with the idea of 400 messages in my inbox when I get back. It's the same problem I have with Mother's Day. You refrain from doing any household chores for an entire day, letting yourself be pampered by your family members who insist that you sit and read a book and have your nails done while someone prepares burnt toast and lukewarm tea, and then you wake up the next morning with twice the laundry and dishes and light-bulbs-to-be-changed awaiting you, because of course no one has thought to do any of that during your sabbatical of a day.

It makes you wonder if it's worth it.

I also can't quite imagine being away from my blog for a week, especially when there will be so much to tell.

Maybe what I need for my packing list is a super-light netbook running on solar power and thin air.

Max – who, at the latest, is still coming – will have his own demons to battle with. How to survive without a sink and soap to wash his hands every time a speck of real or imagined dirt lands on them? No Xbox for an entire week? No reading up on soccer league scores? No alone time, for that matter?

Another thing I absolutely know I will struggle with is speed. I'm not worried about not being fast enough, but rather the opposite: slowing myself down enough to beat altitude sickness. Everything I do, I do fast. I can't help myself.

I rush through dinner prep.

I type like there is no tomorrow.

I speak fast.

It drives me absolutely crazy when people walk super-slow in front of me, blocking the way, something that seems to happen particularly often in Africa. Don't they have any place they want to get to? Anything to check off their to-do lists? Isn't there always something better to do with your time than walk?

I'm also very competitive. If someone is running next to me, I want to beat them. This served me well as a kid when kicking the soccer ball as the lone girl in a group of boys, or when taking up basketball at the rather advanced age of 17. But my urge to win can have rather ridiculous outgrowths, some of them counterproductive. Do I really need to be the best at arranging plates in the dishwasher? Do I really need to win every family croquet game? And, after breaking my wrist a few years ago, did I really have to take my physical therapy exercises to such a level that my left wrist is now more flexible than my right?

I know that it won't be easy, but somehow I will have to rein in this need to hurry, to come in first, or I will thwart my chances of reaching the summit. Slowing myself down is the single most important thing I am told I can do to make it all the way up. The slower you go, the better your chances. *Pole pole*. From the moment you conduct your first research about Mount Kilimanjaro, you'll come across those two words. *Pole pole* (*poh*-leh *poh*-leh) is Swahili and means slowly, steadily, one step at a time. It should be seen not only as a literal admonishment to walk slowly, but as an entire philosophy of slowing down our lives, focusing on the here and now, stopping to smell the roses. And trusting that you can almost always take just one more step, whatever the challenge.

Maybe this is precisely what we need: to leave behind our comfort zones, live without the things we seem to cherish so much, and dramatically slow down the pace. Just for a week. The packing list seems to agree with this. There are absolutely no electronics on it, which I guess is a good thing. Life is so much easier if you don't have to worry about chargers, batteries, and other gadgets. I will be taking a camera, because I couldn't imagine not chronicling this most adventurous of adventures in pictures, and I might bring a second one just in case, but that will be it.

No netbook for me, solar or otherwise.

And time to stop fretting about our climb, whether it features garden trowels or not. Instead of wondering how hard it might be, I should be looking forward to the thrill of it.

The biggest thrill, I am surprised to realize, might very well be that I will undertake it together with my son.

The Test Hike

May 2012, four months to go

Only four months left until September: it's time to go on a
test hike. We need to get our shoes broken in.

And, in the words of Mike (who as chief organizer
has emerged as the leader of our group), we need to
"toughen up" in preparation for the real thing.
Toughening up, according to Mike, is best achieved by
carrying 12 kilograms on our backs when we do our test
hike. "Bring your daypack – packed to 12kg – use bricks
wrapped in newspaper if required" was the exact wording
in one of his emails to the group. But we find it cruel
enough to have to show up at the crack of dawn at
Groenkloof Nature Reserve, so our family politely declines
on the brick option.

Besides, I'm not entirely convinced we need to go test
hiking in preparation for Kilimanjaro, with or without
bricks. Yes, the boots should be broken in, and hiking
helps with that. And yes, you should walk fairly regularly,
and when in this day and age do we ever take a walk if
we're not going hiking? And yes, there is absolutely
nothing wrong with regular walks even if you don't plan
on scaling a mountain. And finally, anywhere you go with
Mike promises to be fun, especially since there'll probably
be one mishap or another, judging by his highly

entertaining battle stories. Going on a test hike should be good entertainment if nothing else.

But it's only because of the prospect of fun that I'm coming along. My philosophy – and it has served me fairly well in life – is to avoid doing unpleasant things in preparation for something unpleasant. For instance, would you go to the dentist and have him inflict a little bit of pain on you, with increasing weekly doses, just to prepare you for the big event of taking out your wisdom teeth? "Just another little push, ma'am, and then we'll be at about 70 percent of how it will feel after we're done with you." Or would you, before ever conceiving children, go to some kind of childbirth simulator where you could experience what it feels like? I don't think so. Some things are better left unknown. If I have to feel exhausted and tired and cold for the duration of the week that I'll be climbing Kili, so be it. But I don't feel the need to add any exhaustion and tiredness to my plate right now.

For this reason I have totally disregarded the physical training program that was attached to one of Mike's emails. Drawn up by Kilimanjaro experts, it outlines gym sessions on the Stairmaster and treadmill and stationary bike, and leg presses and sit-ups and knee extensions, complemented by daily walks and 20-kilometer hikes in between those, for a total of about 25 hours per day once you add it all up. The best part is this: They want you to hike in hilly terrain so that you can reproduce as closely as possible what awaits you on the mountain, as long as you avoid going downhill so as to protect the knees. I'm not entirely sure how it's possible to hike up and down hills without in fact going down them, but maybe that's just me.

I'm not an expert.

I happen to think a hiking regime doesn't greatly enhance your chances of success, if success indeed means you want to make it to the summit. Altitude sickness is the number one reason why people have to turn back prematurely, not a lack of physical fitness. And, as the name suggests, it's caused by exposure to extreme altitudes. Or, as Mike put it in one of his emails, "Acute Mountain Sickness (AMS) can be fatal and will definitely ruin your chances of summiting." I daresay the part about it being fatal would indeed ruin your chances of summiting. In a fatal kind of way.

You can't really prepare for altitude sickness, other than understanding what it is and watching for the symptoms. Unless of course you buy the *Mountain Air Generator* I've come across online, "direct over the web, all major credit cards accepted, 30-day money-back guarantee" for "only" 2,500 dollars. All you have to do, if I'm to believe the glowing testimonials on this company's website, is set up the dome over the head end of your bed ("room for two available"), plug it into the oxygen or rather reverse oxygen machine, and breathe in the thin mountain air every night over the course of a few weeks or even months. After completing such a regimen, you can apparently saunter up the mountain without a care in the world because you'll be fully acclimatized. The only problem is that in all likelihood you won't get an opportunity to saunter up the mountain at all, because your spouse, after three days of sharing the bed with a wheezing machine and an oxygen tent, has almost certainly killed you.

Perhaps it's more advisable to go about this the old-fashioned and time-tested way. Because in a fashion, altitude sickness is not a sickness at all. On the contrary, your body in the most amazing manner is able to adapt to high-altitude conditions if given enough time. You know those little thingies that fall down from the ceiling in an airplane in the event of a loss of air pressure, the ones you're supposed to put on yourself first and then the small children? At least that's what I think I remember from the time before I started tuning out the annoying safety talk sometime in 1991. Well, you better hustle to put on those masks in order to breathe, is what I've just learned. According to the book *Altitude Illness: Prevention and Treatment*, you have about four minutes before you lose consciousness, and then you die. But many people climbing at about the same altitude when they scale mountains like Mount Everest quite successfully do so without dying or even losing consciousness (Reinhold Messner was the first to conquer Everest without oxygen). How can this be?

It's called acclimatization. Somehow your body responds to the lower levels of oxygen, if given enough time, by gradually speeding up the process of getting oxygen into your blood and moving it around to where it's needed. The very first sign of it is that you start breathing faster, whether it's conscious or not. At extreme altitude (anything over 5,500 meters) you sound like a marathon runner even when you're sitting in an armchair doing nothing. People who call their loved ones from the highest camp on Kilimanjaro or even the summit will tell you that the first words on the other end, in all likelihood, are "What have you been doing? You sound like you've just run a 100-meter sprint!"

Not only does your breathing increase, but also your heart rate. Which is why you might see some people sitting in front of their tents at higher altitudes with a contraption on their finger measuring their pulse. I'm not sure what you're supposed to do with that information, but I guess it must convey some level of comfort knowing that you still have a pulse. Oh, and another response to high altitude is diuresis (that's a fancy way of saying you have to pee a lot). Also, your blood thickens (probably because you pee so much), and that is most decidedly not a good thing because it can lead to blood clots which can kill you. Some people recommend taking aspirin to counter blood thickening, but opinions are divided on its effectiveness.

The most noticeable change in your body caused by increasing altitude is your inability to sleep, or at least to sleep well. Whenever your brain detects too little oxygen while you're sleeping, it tells you to wake up ASAP, which I suppose is a good thing. Sleeping pills, by the way, have the effect of slowing down your breathing and are therefore a terrible idea when hiking at altitude.

Altitude sickness is what happens when your body is telling you that this has all become too much. That you've climbed too fast, and that it can't make these adjustments quickly enough. That if you turn right around and go down, down, down, everything will be just dandy again. The lower concentration of oxygen at high elevations is not the only problem. What also happens – and I don't think it is entirely understood why – is that the lower air pressure makes fluid leak from your capillaries, which in turn can cause dangerous levels of fluid build-up in your lungs and brain. The latter will definitely kill you if left unattended.

There is a long list of things you can do to prevent the onset of altitude sickness or at least keep symptoms to a minimum. All I've remembered is "climb high, sleep low." And that it's not a good idea to fly into a high-elevation destination and go even higher the very next day. I don't think we'll be at risk of that, given that we'll be "trikkin walking," according to Mike, for an entire week.

Our family does have a little bit of experience with the "climb high, sleep low" mantra, if only due to our complete disregard of it. Klaus and I had been skiing in Europe as well as the U.S. for years before we had children, and it never occurred to us that elevation might have to be a consideration when booking a trip (other than making sure you got the most fantastic and reliable snow.) Altitude never bothered us. As our family expanded, and as we first started taking our kids on ski trips, it became a curious side note that our children happened to catch some sort of stomach ailment during every trip. We always blamed it on the food or flu season or both. Our eyes were finally opened by a conscientious ski school instructor in Breckenridge, CO, who encouraged us to take two of our kids straight to the clinic after they'd been barfing all over the slope that morning in his class. It was such a light bulb moment for us, and while we were sitting around hospital beds receiving instructions on the proper use of an oxygen machine, we regaled each other with tales of family ski vacations since 1998 which had all featured puking kids in one way or another. Come to think of it, maybe this is why the kids have always hated ski school so much; it probably felt more like spew school to them.

This is how I know that "climb high, sleep low" is important, and that Breckenridge, at 2,900 meters of altitude, does not qualify as "low." To summit Kilimanjaro, we will have to go nearly twice as high. I'll gladly leave the exact details of where and how much I climb each day to the people who'll be guiding us. They're the experts. The trick is to correctly read the symptoms of altitude sickness so that you don't mistake it for some other ailment and carry on climbing. I suppose in this respect it does help to test yourself beforehand to see how you might respond, but it is just a tad difficult to find a suitable high-altitude location for your Sunday stroll just around the corner from where you live.

Groenkloof Nature Reserve is right next to Pretoria and indeed just around the corner from where we live. But in the nature department it's as far removed from Mount Kilimanjaro as you can get. The city is all around us and at first we can't even have a conversation because there is so much traffic noise. Not that I could have much of a conversation anyway with all that huffing and puffing I am doing just to keep up. What happened to *pole pole*?

We've barely rounded the first bend when we are treated to an entirely different sight: giraffes grazing

serenely on the side of the path. That's what I love about
living in Africa. You can always rely on some cool animal
sightings, even if you've practically just dodged a minibus
taxi careening around the corner.

Klaus is sauntering ahead, and to use the opportunity
for the good one-on-one talks that so often elude us at
home with four children in the house, I hustle to keep up
with him. I admire his energy and wonder once again
why, exactly, he won't be doing the real hike with us. We
are deep in conversation when something makes us stop
and turn around. There, on the horizon, is the rest of our
group, everyone frantically waving their arms and moving
their mouths in what looks like shouts of "come back!"

It seems we have managed to get lost a mere 20
minutes into our test hike. I make a mental note not to
stray so far from our guides when scaling Kili. I am
terrible at directions.

It's fun hiking in a group, because you can realign
yourself with different people every once in a while to
switch conversations. And to see what kind of candy they
brought. I'm notorious in my family for never bringing
any cool food. I can barely be bothered to prepare some
water bottles. I simply hate packing, and I hate the
packing of food more than anything else. You do not want
to go on a picnic with me, unless you cater for yourself.
Not only do I barely manage to smother a few slices of
bread with peanut butter and – on good day – throw in a
few apples, I also never bring any kind of utensil that
might be useful, like paper plates for the food.

The only way I can be convinced to pack any food is
cost. As in *holy-cow-these-lunch-prices-are-insane* cost. I hate
to pack a lunch, but I hate to pay top dollar for a few
chicken fingers even more. The time we took the children
to Disney World in Florida, I had everyone prepare some
bagels with cream cheese at the breakfast buffet every
morning, grab a few bananas, and off we we'd go. I almost
had a bagel mutiny on my hands by the end of the week.

Even Klaus, who is usually pleased about any kind of savings when we travel, was dying for a good old hamburger after Day Three.

Some in our Kili group are already scheming to see how many snacks they can bring while staying within the 15 kilogram limit, but I couldn't care less. Whatever it is those porters are toting up the mountain for us, I will happily eat. Or not. Just as long as I don't have to do any food planning for a week.

That's possibly the one thing I get most excited about regarding our Kili climb.

And if this test hike is any indication, I will not want for any snacks on the big mountain. We have food to feed a small army, and we are barely gone for four hours. Even so, we make it a priority to find a place for brunch afterwards where we relax over coffee and scones (and, I have to say, a few beers) while exchanging battle stories, which no one can tell quite as well as a true South African. Klaus and I are the main characters in one such story. Why can't we read signs, we are asked? Without the others yelling and waving us back, we might have led them in a totally wrong direction, they complain, and everybody would still be walking on sore feet instead of eating this well-earned meal in the warm sunshine!

So what's the outcome of the test hike, you might ask? Well. Outcome number one is that we have resolved to do these regularly as much as time allows with our busy schedules. I'm sure the main motivation for some of us is not the prospect of getting fitter, but the prospect of another brunch with beer and good jokes.

Outcome number two is that I'm now fairly confident that I will enjoy the real thing, especially without the Voortrekker Monument in the background. I know I'll be utterly exhausted, if a mere four hours without bricks is anything to judge by. I fear that my left Achilles tendon will give me trouble because it's hurting like hell at the moment, but I'm blaming it on the stiff new boots. Just to be aware of this now has made the test hike worthwhile. I know I will enjoy the good company and the views and yes, the fresh air. I will enjoy taking pictures. Taken with a small camera, I'm afraid, because lugging the big Canon uphill was no picnic.

Oh, and I never got to check out the toilet situation, which I still can't get my mind off of.

Especially the *female* toilet situation.

Peequality: The Last Frontier of Women's Equality

May 2012, three and a half months to go

I've just gotten an email from my friend Sharon, who will also be one of the climbers in our group, giving us tips from a female friend of hers who just came back from Kili. Getting such tips from someone who recently returned is always the most welcome information because, you figure, the fresher the better.

As soon as the kids are off to school, I pour myself a cup of tea and read through everything with rapt attention. The friend's advice is mainly about making sure our sleeping bags are warm enough and how to best pack our clothes, which is nothing much new to me. But then Sharon writes this: "*For the ladies she recommends getting the travel rest stop urination bags as a better option to the 'Shewee'.*"

I've never heard of a Shewee but it doesn't require all that much imagination to guess what *she* together with *wee* does. I am immediately intrigued. It must be a device similar to the "Urinelle" that I stumbled across online a few weeks ago. I've been watching and re-watching the Brazilian promotional video for it ever since then, and I've shared it with all my friends. I've practically become addicted to it. It's a fascinating concept and the advertisement is hilarious, featuring a woman contorting herself in all sorts of ways to avoid touching a succession of dirty toilet seats, dramatic music building in the background with each new attempt, until the Urinelle practically comes riding to the rescue in shining armor to save the day, allowing the (very hot) woman to stand right next to some guy at the urinal and pee through a long hose, the front end discreetly tucked under her skirt. I think it ends with the guy fainting. Go on, watch it on YouTube, I know you want to!

I thought this was just an off-the-wall joke product when I got the link in an email from a Brazilian relative, but apparently the Urinelle is not the only one of its kind. On the contrary, it seems to have quite a few competitors. Perhaps these things do have merit. I recall more than one instance when my dear husband thought it was amusing to snap pictures of my bare bottom on the few occasions I've found myself out in the woods with my pants around my ankles.

Intrigued by this whole new market of products I'm not sure what to call, I drop everything I've been doing and set out to conduct more research. I can't find the "travel rest stop urination bags" (don't ask what I *do* find for that search term – there is an entire world out there revolving around "travel rest stop" and "urination" that I'm not sure I want to learn more about), so I go on to the Shewee, "the original female urine device since 1999," even if that's the one *not* recommended by Sharon's friend. It looks like a stunted funnel and can be had, for only $15.97, with an "extension pipe" that is "great for extra reach when aiming into a Peebol."

Of course, only a woman could be enticed to spend money on a device to improve her aim into the bowl because her original device leaves something to be desired. If only men could be made to carry extension pipes around with them, then toilets the world over would be a happier place.

The Shewee website is full of other intriguing nuggets of wisdom. "Stand up and take control" is the company slogan. Pretty good marketing, if you ask me. The device itself comes in three different colors: one for "the outdoor girl who just likes to get on with the guys on whatever adventure or challenge is set" (green); one for "the ladies who just love to shout about Shewee and are proud to be who they are" (pink); and one for "the more discreet lady who simply wants to stay clean and hydrated in her day to day life whether she's driving for work or a shopping trip only offers dirty public toilets" (white).

How to pick the right one? Those are entirely too many choices for me right there. I can't even choose between two scents of dishwashing soap on a grocery shelf in under ten minutes. But I don't think I could go for white. I mean, that woman who can't manage to use the toilet *before* driving to work so that she won't have to go *while* driving to work – where the hell does she work, Antarctica? Or else she has an extremely small bladder. I know I don't want to be *that* kind of woman. But do I want to shout out proudly about Shewee by going pink? More importantly, who would I shout it out proudly to? I wouldn't want to be fumbling around my crotch and somehow attaching some plastic device in plain view of anybody else. Nothing left but going with army green and "getting on with the guys," especially since we are indeed going on an adventure. I make a mental note to check with Mike and the three other men in our group if purchasing a green Shewee and joining them for a communal pee would fall into the "getting on with them" category. I don't think I should mention it to the younger set of guys, namely the three teenage boys, or I'll run the risk that Max will never talk to me again.

Come to think of it, I would suggest the Shewee people add a glow-in-the-dark version to the selection. For "when you step out of your tent at night and want to pee against it while standing up without having to don a headlamp to make sure you don't accidentally have the spout feeding into your pant leg."

Now I'm on a roll. What else is out there, I wonder?

What's out there is a surprisingly large variety catering to every buyer group and subgroup imaginable. There seems to be something on offer for everyone. Everyone, that is, as long as she's a woman. The basic flaw with this entire product line, you see, is that it services only half the population. A good marketer would expand their target audience.

This is where the "pStyle" comes in. "The pStyle is a device that allows women and trans men to pee standing up without undressing" proclaims the pStyle website. Without taking any stand here – no pun intended – you do wonder how many transgender customers this tagline gets them. If you used to have a perfectly fine and easy-to-operate device attached to your body to pee standing up, and then you have that device surgically removed, and then you go out looking for products that might allow you to pee standing up, are you out of your fucking mind?

Some more research reveals that the generic term I've been looking for is "Female Urination Device" or FUD. If nothing else, this market seems to be a haven for witty taglines. "Don't take life sitting down," proclaims the website for "GoGirl," an FUD that seems to have cornered the American market. It seems to be one of the better ones out there in terms of sealing seamlessly against your skin. It boasts a "splash guard" and has the benefit of being disposable (an American specialty). Although I reckon that might pose a slight problem during a Kili hike, as I try to picture the hillside dotted with little purple silicone hats along the trails. The folks at GoGirl will also have you know that while the idea of an FUD might be alien to you, European women have been doing it that way for years. Years! This is news to me. Being a European woman myself, this particular trend seems to have entirely passed me by. Hats off to the GoGirl marketing team: they've made urination fashionable. I can totally see the scene in my mind: Elaine, calling after Jerry Seinfeld: "It's not an FUD, it's *European!*"

The website for "Magic Cone" (30 cones for 25 Canadian dollars), which mainly seems to attract grammatically challenged testimonial givers, offers yet another nifty FUD: one that has the advantage of folding flat for easy stowing in your purse as well as being biodegradable. It also gives out helpful hints, should you not be clear whether you belong in their target group or not. You might not have realized it, but you probably are. Dog walkers, for instance, are ideal candidates, as are festival and concert goers. Just in case you want to help your dog feel less embarrassed while he's doing his business by doing yours alongside him. Ditto for the guy next to you at the open-air concert. The festival cone comes as a dual-use edition with a little lighter attached to it so that you can hold up and wave a flame during your favorite songs. Okay, I made that last one up. Golfers are also listed (because while it's totally not socially acceptable to squat down and pee onto the green, discreetly stepping to the side and watering the bunker through your Magic Cone will not raise any eyebrows – just make sure you use the little rake to straighten out the sand afterwards), as are scuba divers. (How do the physics of that one work out, I wonder?) The one genuinely practical reference I can find on their website is the one about "women giving urine samples." I could have made good use of the Magic Cone throughout four pregnancies' worth of doctors' visits, had I had one then.

Also praised as particularly useful for festival goers is the "P EZ Female Urinal." I don't know about this obsession with festivals, but it's enough for me to never want to attend one again. You're practically guaranteed to be assaulted from all sides by women exercising their newfound freedom in liquid form, if I am to believe all this advertising. According to Amazon, The P EZ "allows women of all ages to pee in a standing up, sitting down, or lying position without undressing." This is getting better and better. Apparently, we do not only want the freedom to relieve ourselves while standing up, we also want it while lying down. Although I'm fairly certain this will not work. It's simple physics. Reviewer number three seems to agree with me. "The only downside I see with this product is that it does not allow you to direct the flow away from your body," she writes. Yep, that is a slight problem, isn't it?

Finally, there is the "P-Mate," another disposable variety which promises an end to women losing their dignity. It might not win the style contest – it rather looks like a cross between one of those paper cones you might purchase candied almonds in and a Dutch wooden shoe – but what's absolutely best about the P-Mate is that it finally – *finally* – allows women to write their names in the snow with their pee. With dignity! I know this because I've watched the video on the website with my own eyes. To think that women have now reached this pinnacle of equality after centuries – no, millennia – of their struggle for equal rights is enough to make a grown woman pee in her pants.

I admit it's that last one that almost – almost – has me drop a pack into the online shopping cart, strictly for research purposes of course. I sort of want to practice my snow-pee-doodling skills. Besides, what a powerful message to take a pack up Kili and hand it out to the other women, then form a line and immortalize our collective urine in the Furtwängler Glacier. Come to think of it, I wonder if I should contact the company and offer to become their Kilimanjaro spokesperson. Who needs a charitable cause for climbing Kili when they can make a few bucks hawking FUDs instead?

In the end, the question of "FUD – yes or no?" seems to evoke similar images in my mind as the garden trowel for our ablutions. Because what remains is the somewhat disquieting debate of clean-up-before-stowing-away versus stowing-away-without-cleanup, and quite frankly I'm not inclined to explore either one of these options any further. Even though what I've seen does pique my curiosity, I'm still leaning toward the traditional approach for my ablutions on the mountain, otherwise known as pulling down your pants and squatting behind a boulder.

I've never been an early adopter of new technology.

Although I *would* like to be able to say I Shewee'd – yes, it is a verb, I checked – on Kilimanjaro.

Just Give Me a Mountain

June 2012, three months to go

Yesterday I realized that our Kili trip is inching uncomfortably close. I was standing with a few other mothers at Sharon's horse stable – she runs an equestrian therapy center focusing on disadvantaged and disabled children, supplemented by the income from after-school riding classes – while we were waiting for our daughters to be finished with their lesson, and one of them, having heard that I was preparing for a Kili climb, proceeded to quiz me on every detail. She had formerly lived in Tanzania, which gave her at least partial authority on the topic.

"When are you going?"

Gulp. "Errr – first week of September," I volunteered.

"Wow, how awesome, that's coming up soon!" she chirped.

What, soon? I did a quick calculation in my head. Our trip was starting in three months. In theory, that sounds like plenty of time, but I have quite a few projects to tackle before then.

One of them is my diary. Back in February I had visions of conducting a ton of research so that I could update my diary with all sorts of cool facts about Kilimanjaro, but so far all I can show in terms of research are the various uses of a garden trowel and instructions on how to pee into a Urinelle. If the chronicles of my

adventure are to be more than just an advertisement for
female urination devices, then I better get my act together.

Also, I still have to make a doctor's appointment for
altitude sickness and malaria medication, apply for
Tanzanian visas, buy a couple of duffel bags, and check
my list for anything else that's still missing. I don't even
want to think of all the daily walking in my hiking boots I
am supposed to have done. And all of this needs to be
completed sooner rather than later, because we will be
gone two weeks in August for what will be our last
African family vacation – two weeks that will be missing
from my Kili prep time.

All this was racing through my head as I stood there
chatting with these other moms in the afternoon sun and
after the word "soon" had triggered a minor panic attack
in me. All of a sudden, my three months were starting to
feel awfully busy. I made a mental note to write a Kili to-
do list as soon as I got home. I always feel better after
writing a long list.

But my interrogation clearly wasn't over.

"Which airport are you flying into?"

At this I opened my mouth and then closed it again. I
had no idea which airport we were flying into. I barely
even knew that Mount Kilimanjaro is in Tanzania. I
consulted my brain to see if I knew any cities in Tanzania.

I didn't.

"You know, where all the people who are climbing
Kili fly into," I pronounced with all the confidence I could
muster. All I knew was that someone booked plane tickets
for us. I didn't even know who *that* was, if I'm completely
honest.

"Oh, I'm so excited for you," she went on. "So what
route will you be climbing?"

Wait... I used to know this. There was definitely
mention of a route. Of which we were taking the longer
one, I did remember that. To better acclimatize. They all
have complicated names which I can't remember,

although some of them have nicknames, which I do remember, like the Coca-Cola Route and the Whiskey Route.

I've been hoping they'll open up a Chardonnay one, myself.

The cross-examination *still* wasn't finished. The next thing my interrogator wanted to know, of all the possible things one might want to know, was whether we were climbing Kili during a full moon. I was so taken aback that I was speechless. I don't know when there is a full moon at the best of times, until I happen to notice it right there in the sky, and it usually makes me happy to see it, but that's it. I certainly don't think I've ever planned a vacation according to the moon cycle. The monsoon cycle perhaps, but not the moon. I'm already stressed out enough having to factor in when the kids are out of school or when I can get a babysitter, and so any astronomical considerations don't usually enter my mind. For this Kilimanjaro venture I remember that my only concern was when the weather was most suitable to climb up 6,000 meters – because frankly, full moon or not, I would rather not die of hypothermia in a seasonal snowstorm. Forgive me, but the moon is rather far down on my priority list, along with the TV Guide for the first week of September.

However, bright moonlight during summit night is apparently a coveted commodity among Kili experts. Had I bothered to do any research, I might have come across this particular aspect of our climb. Thankfully, I was rescued before having to reveal my ignorance about the September moon phases. Sharon, who had come over to chat with us and had caught the last part of the conversation, cut off any further questions with an authoritative "Don't ask us all these technical questions. We'll just show up where they tell us and start walking. Just give us a mountain."

And it's true. Those are exactly my sentiments. In fact, I'm secretly looking forward to the Kili trip, even though I'm publicly pretending to be scared of the challenge. In reality it has all the trappings of a dream vacation: beyond lacing up my boots in the morning, I won't have to plan my day.

I won't have to do any shopping.

I won't have to cook any meals.

I won't even have to *plan* any meals.

I won't have to urge anybody along, other than myself.

I won't have to answer any questions beyond "Are you going to have the tea or the coffee" upon dragging myself into camp each afternoon.

I won't have to think about anything. The only thing I will have to think about is which might be the best spot for my you-know-what and whether it was really necessary to schlepp along that garden trowel urged onto me by my packing list. I will have hours at my disposal to contemplate that single question, and that thought, irrationally, makes me happy.

It's not that I never plan ahead. It's just that I don't have a strong need to know the precise step-by-step plan. I'm quite happy to trust others, especially those who are professionals in their fields. But I'm sure there are people who will have read that *Guide to Kilimanjaro* cover to cover and will have agonized over the benefits and drawbacks of all the different routes, which outfitter to pick, which hotel to stay at. Typically, given my luck, I'm paired with one of those people on my first day, and they'll then proceed to describe to me, in minute detail, all the things that can possibly go wrong.

Of course there is also the other kind of traveler, the one who you wish *had* read the memo, because just as you're about to start walking they have a million questions. Like *What if we can't go on,* or *How will we know we can't go on,* and *Will somebody climb back down the mountain with us if we can't go on*?

When Klaus and I toured Victoria Falls some time back, we had an American couple of that type in our canoeing group. We had spent all morning taking shuttles to the starting point, signing indemnity forms, and listening to endless instructions. When we were just about to finally step into the mighty Zambezi – can you imagine the glorious moment? – the questions started. Like "Wait a minute, let me see if I got this right – if you want to turn to the right, you paddle on the left like this?" and the woman would demonstrate her technique to our guide. "And then like this to turn left?" and again she would demonstrate, that time paddling through the air on her right.

For more than 20 minutes she and her husband continued to pepper our poor guide with their concerns, like *what if we get attacked by a hippo, what if we get attacked by a crocodile, is there anything else we might be attacked by, when will we be picked up again, where precisely will we be picked up again, where will we be brought from there, how long will it take before we have the first break, where can we put our camera, do you have a waterproof bag, do we EACH get a waterproof bag...?* The fact that they were dressed up in matching his-and-her safari gear (or what someone shopping on Fifth Avenue in New York might consider to be proper safari gear) didn't help. By the time we finally got going, Klaus and I were rather hoping we would indeed be attacked by a ferocious beast with an appetite for New Yorkers asking too many questions.

I find "What if?" the most tiresome question there is. I have a child who can spend hours quizzing me on what-if scenarios. One time we vacationed with friends and she agonized during the entire weekend over whether she wanted to sleep out in the open next to a camp fire with the other kids on our final night or back at the lodge with the adults. She drove me absolutely insane with her indecision on the issue, trying to weigh every what-if angle there was and somehow always involving me in the deliberations, and in the end we accidentally set the bush on fire (yes, we did, and we're not proud of it), and no sleep was to be had after that, neither at the fire nor in the house. All of a sudden, we had a *real* problem to tackle.

All that fretting over nothing.

When she now comes to me with similar worries, all I have to say is "remember the fire" to stop her from uttering any what-ifs.

My philosophy is more one of "let's get started and answer questions along the way." Much like you eventually have to get going with a new board game to truly comprehend it, rather than sitting there for hours reading the instructions. It usually becomes clear along the way.

Nothing is more tiresome than exploring a new place with a crowd and endlessly debating the merits of this restaurant or that, for instance, when all you want to do is start walking wherever your feet might carry you. Or perhaps I'm just in denial and my real problem is that I can't make any decisions. As in, *do I bring the blue t-shirt or the white?* I *hate* packing. Klaus will attest to that, because he hears me complain about it at every turn. I also don't like taking charge and am quite happy to follow the crowd like a sheep. This is why it was such a brilliant plan to find a group to join for this Kili hike, a group that includes the *Energizer Bunny* in human form, someone who is walking around with bricks in his backpack to prepare for the climb.

I have not been walking around with bricks in my backpack. I have not been walking around much even without bricks, come to think of it. And I have not been observing the phases of the moon.

But I am confident that once we get there it will be fairly obvious what I must do.

Just give me a mountain!

Which Country Are We Flying to Again?

Not only have I gladly ceded most of the planning for our trip to someone else, I also haven't bothered yet to do any kind of research. I know as much about Mount Kilimanjaro as I know about the life cycle of earth worms. And it's not due to my lack of interest but rather my lack of time. With four kids in the house, I've got enough stuff to keep busy with, and any attempt to steal a few quiet moments with a book or on my computer is often thwarted by some kind of emergency.

Take this morning for instance. It started with a piercing scream from upstairs, going something like "Mooooooom, I can't find my tracksuit pants," prompting me to abandon my just-poured cup of tea and hurry upstairs, only to be diverted by "My tracksuit top is goooooooone!" from another direction. One of the joys of living in South Africa is the fact that the children attend school in uniforms, simplifying many aspects of our life considerably, but one drawback is that I have to constantly deal with lost and misplaced pieces of clothing. I spent the next ten minutes rummaging through closets and laundry baskets, defending the at that time still absent housekeeper who inevitably gets blamed for things not put in the right place. The mere suggestion on my part that the tracksuit pants might have been forgotten at school last week resulted in a barrage of verbal abuse the likes of which only one's own child can emit, even though every bit of past evidence pointed at precisely such a scenario. We have single-handedly kept that school uniform store in business over the past two years with all the replacements we've had to buy. I refrained from saying "That's why I tell you to put all your stuff out the night before," because experience has taught me that this is generally not very well received and contributes nothing to the ultimate goal, which in this case was to get the kids out the door. My choices were sending one girl into the freezing cold with a jacket and short pants and the other with long pants but no jacket, or sending one out fully clad and the other one more or less naked. That might have been a good natural consequence if it hadn't turned out that the missing pants were the housekeeper's fault after all. I spotted Max walking out the house with them a short while later, totally oblivious of the fact that they barely reached below his knee and must have been put in his closet by mistake.

If it's not lost clothing, it's something else that spices up our mornings. A dog-eared form that has spent the better part of a week in one of the boys' backpacks needing to be filled out with all sorts of data "absolutely, positively today, Mom, or I'll get in trouble." Or one of the girls crying amidst a sea of socks and claiming that every single one "feels weird and doesn't fit." Or, my favorite, 15 pictures to be printed out before school for some family history timeline project, which never fails to be the precise moment the printer's ink cartridge has run out, the paper is jammed, or the spooler full.

And so the rest of my day typically goes. But in the interest of learning more about the place Max and I are flying to in less than two months, and so that I can better answer any future questions about where we're flying to, I have been carving out some precious time to dig up more information.

Mount Kilimanjaro is in Tanzania. Or rather, it sort of straddles Kenya and Tanzania. Nairobi in Kenya is the closest big airport you can fly into, but most of the mountain, including its summit, lies in Tanzania. This means that Tanzania has three great things going for it (which is only fair considering it's one of the world's poorest countries): Mount Kilimanjaro, the annual wildebeest migration in the Serengeti, and the island of Zanzibar. In fact, some travelers combine two or even all three of these into one gigantic trip.

The Serengeti is something I'm afraid my family and I will never get to experience, given that a tented safari for six including an excursion into the Ngorongoro Crater costs the equivalent of a small house. But we have, in fact, been to Zanzibar. What lured us there was the exotic name. And the fact that Freddie Mercury was born there. I admit that I didn't know this before we booked our vacation, but I've been dazzling a lot of people with that tidbit of trivia ever since.

My lasting impression of Zanzibar, aside from the haunting beauty of wooden dhows gliding across the setting sun, was *hakuna matata*. If there is one phrase that encompasses not just the people of Tanzania but the entire Swahili culture, it is *hakuna matata*. It means something close to "no worries," as immortalized in the movie *The Lion King*, but until our Zanzibar vacation I didn't know that these words were actually spoken by real people other than Elton John.

You didn't have to know much Swahili to have a conversation in Zanzibar, which would always go something like this:

"Jambo" (*How are you?*)
"Sijambo" (*I am well*)
"Hakuna matata."

Every encounter ended with *hakuna matata*, and coupled with the brilliant smile most Zanzibaris offered you, it soon started to seep into your psyche. There is no reason to worry! Life is great! Everything will work out! Of course it helps when you're lodging at a five-star resort with free round-the-clock drinks to your heart's content, but still. Montaigne once said that "the pleasantest things in the world are pleasant thoughts: and the great art of life is to have as many of them as possible." If anyone has taken this advice to heart, it is the people of Zanzibar and, by extension, the rest of Tanzania and Kenya as well. *Hakuna matata* goes a long way toward keeping pleasant thoughts in your mind.

Tanzania has quite the interesting history. Or perhaps it's mainly interesting to someone with a German background like me. I always love to hear of countries the Germans once conquered or at least made an effort to conquer. I know that this is quite irrational, because I dislike the very idea of conquering and meddling in someone else's business.

But it's a little bit like the Olympics: you just have to win the medal count!

Not that the Germans, always late to the party, distinguished themselves much in the geopolitical medal count. And where they did appear, they mainly distinguished themselves at making particularly bad choices.

I mean, Swakopmund, of all places?

If you've ever made your way to Swakopmund, tucked away on the windswept Atlantic coast of Namibia, you'll agree it is one of the most godforsaken places on Earth. On an entire continent full of lush bush, breathtaking landscapes, and mostly perfect weather, the Germans had to pick the one place with more or less guaranteed fog ten months of the year, occasionally broken up by a sandstorm, along a river that mostly runs dry.

So I'm very interested to learn more about their involvement in Tanzania, on the other side of the African continent. And that is where Mount Kilimanjaro comes in. Apparently, a German missionary by the name of Johannes Rebmann was the first European to set eyes on Mount Kilimanjaro. Although in reality it had been seen and mentioned long before, mainly by Arab traders navigating the waters around Zanzibar. The first reference to a mighty snow-capped mountain somewhere at the source of the Nile might have come from the ancient geographer and astronomer Ptolemy in Alexandria during the second century, though he almost certainly never saw it himself. And then it didn't get mentioned again for over a thousand years. In any case, Rebmann is the one who ended up with the write-up on Wikipedia. Which we all know is the gospel, even if our kids' teachers insist that it can't be trusted.

Rebmann saw and reported of Kilimanjaro in 1848 and was followed into the interior of what became known as Tanganyika by the most illustrious explorers, Richard Burton and Stanley Livingstone among them. But it was another German who laid claim to being the first to summit Kilimanjaro. Remember Dr. Hans Meyer who proved so helpful to me when it came to shopping for equipment? Yes, him. He was the one who stood on Africa's highest point, though he wasn't even sure of it then, in the year 1889.

I daresay he didn't have an easy time of it. His first attempt failed due to a lack of equipment to overcome the heavy snow and ice – something you won't have to deal with at all nowadays, unless you make the effort to hike past the summit and quite a ways toward what remains of the glaciers. But in Meyer's day the ice cap was extending far below the crater rim, the glaciers were cascading down the slopes, and most of the caldera itself – the large depression on the summit – was completely covered. There would have been no way to carry on past 5,000 meters without pickaxes and crampons and such.

When Meyer returned a year later with better gear, he was thwarted again, that time getting into the middle of some revolt and being taken hostage. He was lucky to escape with his life. A few years earlier, the English missionary Charles New, who distinguished himself by having been the first European to step onto snow in equatorial Africa during his own exploration of Kilimanjaro, had gotten into a skirmish with one of the local Moji (now Moshi) chiefs and was attacked and driven back to the coast where he soon succumbed to his injuries (or died from poor health, I can't be sure).

In Meyer's case, a nice sum of rupees was exchanged to secure his release.

I find all of this fascinating. Who knew the early exploration of Mount Kilimanjaro would make for such a riveting tale of intrigue? Our modern-day endeavor to conquer Kili seems mundane, if not outright boring, in comparison. Nevertheless, I'm very happy that I probably won't have heavy snow, murderous local chieftains, or rupee-demanding kidnappers to contend with.

Three is the charm, so Meyer's next attempt brought success. He might also be the only one who can claim to have scaled all 5,895 meters on foot, as his third Kili expedition started in Mombasa on the Kenyan coast, at sea level. Probably more than 5,895 meters, come to think of it, because I have also read that Kili has been shrinking. It might have been higher than 5,895 meters in Meyer's day.

I've become so fascinated by this 19th century history of Kilimanjaro that I've downloaded Dr. Hans Meyer's very own account of his feat, *Across East African Glaciers: An Account of the First Ascent of Kilimanjaro* onto my Kindle. It reads a bit like the Lewis and Clark expedition. Or perhaps more like an Indiana Jones screenplay (back home in Germany, Meyer was a geography professor in Leipzig; I wonder if he attracted women the way Harrison Ford does). Unlike Lewis, Meyer wasn't sent by his government to pursue geographical research in east Africa but rather "resolved to devote myself and my means to it forthwith." He was the ultimate adventurer, but one with a sense of duty to his country. His reasoning was that since a German (Rebmann) had discovered Kilimanjaro, and another German (Baron von der Decken) had first explored it, it seemed "a national duty that a German should be the first to tread the summit of this mountain," which he suspected was the highest in Africa.

Once again, I can't help but feel like a bit of a loser. Here I've been getting all excited about doing something very hard and rather unusual, or so I thought, but the hardest thing I've had to do so far was make a booking with the click of a mouse and buy a few supplies from a place that caters precisely to what's needed for this trip. I'll have an entire crew at my disposal for making sure I arrive safely at my destination, and I can spend hours sitting at my desk reading about the millions who've come before me. While on the mountain I won't have to put any effort towards measuring and cataloguing and reporting its height and width and topographical features, nor will I have to press any of the indigenous plants into my notebook to take home for botanical analysis. Whatever information I could possibly want regarding my Kili trip is at my immediate disposal. Granted, this easy access sometimes gets me derailed so that hours later I find myself reading about King Wenceslaus III of Bohemia and his untimely death in an outhouse, but overall I can still gather vast amounts of pertinent information in a relatively short time.

Whereas our friend Hans didn't even know if he was indeed climbing the highest mountain in Africa, let alone which approach was the safest. The only thing Meyer had to go by were Rebmann's and von Decken's earlier reports of a snow-capped mountain on the equator. At the time this was treated as almost scandalous, and some renowned geographers wasted no time in loudly ridiculing any "description of a snowstorm on the equator during the hottest season of the year." Not to mention that there was an actual war going on where Meyer was traveling. Furthermore, he had to assemble a team of unknown and untested porters from scratch while taking care that he didn't accidentally take on any slaves without the consent of their masters. (Zanzibar didn't abolish slavery until 1897.)

Another thing I can strike off my list. I'm positive that I won't have to worry about accidentally hiring any slaves. I also don't foresee having to crack my whip to mete out lashes to misbehaving porters.

Getting a team together was no small feat for Meyer, and he took great care in sourcing a good mix of soldiers, local guides, and porters for his third attempt when staging his expedition in Zanzibar. He had been burned on the previous attempt when that team abandoned his entourage in droves, which led to the incident of the kidnapping. "We were overwhelmed and made prisoners, loaded with chains, and thrown into a dark hut, where we were left to lie for some days," he writes nonchalantly, as if he were taking a Sunday stroll.

Even though many such not-exactly-encouraging reports must have reached Europe in those early years of exploration, there seems to have been a bit of a mad rush to summit in the 1870s and 1880s, with quite a few people claiming they had made it, and others questioning their truthfulness. Indeed, it sounds a little like our modern-day squabbles over which iPhone app was first patented by whom, or whether that tennis ball indeed touched the line. For some reason this makes me feel better again. Perhaps Meyer wasn't so removed from our modern world after all. He dealt with the same egos, the same petty complaints, and the same shopping ennui. At the very least, I am happy to report, he seems to have shared my exaggerated affinity for comfortable socks.

Chiefly as a result of Meyer's efforts, but also due to some horse-trading among the European powers that be (from what I can tell, those were Britain and Germany), Mount Kilimanjaro became part of German East Africa in the 1880s. I find this more believable than the other story I read which had Queen Victoria of England giving Kilimanjaro to her grandson, Kaiser Wilhelm II of Germany, as a birthday present.

Either way, the Germans lost it in the end – Kilimanjaro as well as the rest of their African holdings. Even though they fought for it valiantly during World War I (against British, or rather Indian troops commanded by none other than Jan Christiaan Smuts who would later become Prime Minister of the newly formed Union of South Africa, and who also managed to thwart the Germans on the other side of the continent in German Southwest Africa, later Namibia, home to the aforementioned Swakopmund), they were forced to cede what was known as the territory of Tanganyika along with everything else they ceded in the Treaty of Versailles. Tanganyika was eventually united with the island of Zanzibar to become Tanzania.

There are more recent but equally intriguing tidbits of Kilimanjaro history. I've read that in 1989, as part of Meyer's 100-year summit anniversary, an African by the name of Yohani Lauwo was discovered who was believed to have been part of the original ascent. This would have made him about 118 years old at the time. (He went on to live until 1996 or, in keeping with the legend, to the age of 127.)

I'm not quite sure about that one, to be honest. Not the claim that an African was possibly the first person to stand on Kili's summit. In fact, it's quite possible that might be true. But that African in particular? Most of this was based on conjecture and his own claims of climbing

Kili three times before World War I. Let's just say that I've heard enough African tales to know that they never lack a lot of embellishment and padding. What's more, Hans Meyer never mentions any African on the summit. I feel like I've become acquainted enough with Meyer over the course of my research to know that he wouldn't have left such an important detail out of his story. He was quite fond of his porters and guides and never hesitated to mention them by name wherever appropriate. Had Lauwo stood on Kibo that fateful night in 1889, Meyer would have given him his due, I'm sure of it.

But I guess belatedly recognizing an African alongside the Europeans (I forgot to mention that there was also an Austrian alpinist, Ludwig Purtscheller, in Meyer's expedition) was the right thing to do, no matter what his name might be.

Because without the local guides, most of us have no chance, as we're about to learn.

Kili Here We Come

This is it. Our Kili climb is almost upon us.

We just have to finish up the packing, and then, in a few days, Max and I are getting on a plane. At some ungodly hour, because we opted for the budget flight, which seemed a good idea at the time. It will take us closer (if only geographically) to our goal. We're first flying to Nairobi, then to the foot of the big mountain. From there we take a shuttle to some nondescript hotel which is also of the budget variety. It'll probably be a bit of a dump.

Except then it does what all Kilimanjaro base hotels do while you're away on the mountain: within the space of seven days, it is magically transformed into a luxury resort. It will boast such wonders as hot running water! Even more amazingly, a toilet! Electric lights! Privacy! And, most importantly, it will have a bar where you can order a cold beverage. What more can you ask for in life?

At some point in time earlier this week I thought I'd never make it. I'm blaming our busy travel schedule and South Africa for my stress. Squeezing so much exploration into the last few months of our expat assignment made sense at the time we planned it, but it has seriously encroached on the time I should have dedicated to the organization of our Kili trip. And South Africa, I remembered only belatedly, is the world capital of shops that are chronically out of things. Which may or may not be restocked this season. Or, quite possibly, ever.

I was running around like crazy for several days trying to gather the last needed items. Mainly warm clothing – you heard me, I do not enjoy being cold. Also, I was getting last-minute medicines, like Diamox for altitude sickness, which you may or may not have to take, depending on who you talk to. And which I know I should have bought earlier to have time to test it for potential side effects, but didn't. I also stocked up on Imodium, just in case. Although it occurs to me that maybe I could save myself the trouble of lugging that around by taking a mouthful right now. Surely being constipated for seven days is much preferable to the alternative.

I got such obscure things as emergency foil blankets and biodegradable soap that comes in little sheets.

I invested in a headlamp because, unlike a South African, I didn't come out of the womb with one already installed on my forehead.

I bought self-inflating sleeping pads and – a luxury, apparently, as they weren't mentioned on my packing list – self-inflating pillows. I bought rain ponchos, insulated water bottles, and sunscreen. I also bought a new pair of sunglasses with some kind of nifty mechanism that makes the frame adjustable. For some reason the sunglasses give me almost as much outsize pleasure as the socks labeled "left" and "right."

I bought a simple mechanical toothbrush, something I haven't used in decades. Not because I'm afraid my trusted Oral-B electric one won't work on Kili – it holds a charge forever – but because I'm scared shitless that someone will make fun of me if I show up with that at the community washing spot on the first morning.

And I resisted the overpowering urge to buy zip-off pants. For they are the sure sign of the uninitiated tourist – this much I have learned from my Kili research so far. I may not know which country we are flying to, which route we are climbing, or whether there will be a full moon during our ascent, but I did take care to read up on the fashion situation.

And zip-off pants are definitely *so* yesterday.

In addition to all this last-minute shopping, I also had to tackle the small matter of getting my hands on American dollars, for tips for the porters and such. It's a good Africa lesson in general. You never know if some crazy African dictator will finally admit that printing fifty trillion dollar notes doesn't make all that much sense, and that the good old US dollar is a much better vehicle to pay government workers and lure tourists. So the number one item you should pack when leaving America for a new life in Africa is a big wad of dollars. Or euros will also do in a pinch. If you didn't bring them with you, you'll have to source dollars locally. Which in South Africa, due to currency exchange controls (and, frankly, mostly terrible customer service), is always a bit of an errand, involving plenty of the shoulder-shrugging and sighs of "welcome to Africa" that we've become accustomed to over the last few years.

Some time ago, when I had about 500 euros left over from a prior trip to Germany, I thought I'd swing by the bank quickly on my round of errands to pay the money into our South African bank account. Of course I should have known better than harboring hopes of completing any African errand "quickly." When I was finally done, I wasn't sure that I hadn't just bought a house. The documents I needed for what I thought would be a simple transaction included a two-page form filled in with all my personal details, a copy of my passport with the visa page, and an affidavit that I didn't own any foreign assets I was planning to sell while residing in South Africa. It took the better part of an hour before it was all done, which I mostly spent watching the clerk's every move as he retyped the entire form I completed into a computer, printed out a series of receipts, copied my passport and filed the copy away – presumably in some giant vault together with all the other copies they'd already made of my passport on previous visits – and then energetically stamped and stapled everything and handed me my own copy.

When I returned to the bank earlier this week to retrieve South African rands from our account and convert them into US dollars, the procedure was more or less the same in reverse. It had the additional complication that I was asked for my plane ticket, which of course I didn't bring on the first try. In South Africa, you see, you can't just willy-nilly buy foreign currency as your heart desires, unless you can vouch for a bona-fide trip abroad. And you pay dearly in fees for the amount you *are* allowed to convert.

And yet, I suppose it could be worse. At least I don't have to schlepp an entire haberdasher's supply of exquisite cloth and beads and other colorful trinkets with me as a means to trade for supplies with the natives and to appease militant chieftains with lavish presents, as was required of Hans Meyer and all the other 19th century explorers of east Africa.

It's always good to put a little perspective on your hardships.

I've managed to get all these errands finished during the course of this week, which is none too soon. There's nothing like a firm deadline to render you at your most productive. And now, with only two days to go, I can no longer avoid the obvious: it's time to pack.

First, I set out the two brand-new lightweight duffel bags I purchased expressly with the porters' heads in mind. I agonized about the correct size for weeks. Bags are typically advertised in terms of volume (here in South Africa in liters), but the guideline from our outfitter indicates a limit in weight (15 kilograms). How the hell am

I supposed to know how much space 15 kilograms' worth of stuff is going to take up? Only when faced with the real danger of having to hand the porters my underwear and t-shirts piecemeal for lack of a proper vessel to contain them did I overcome my indecision and pick out the bags. Or, rather, I had Julie at Trappers pick the bags for me, one green one and one blue one, and now that they're standing in front of me, they seem absolutely perfect.

I gather every last item I've got tucked away in various corners of the house and dump everything onto our bedroom floor. Not a pretty sight, I can assure you, and one that doesn't fail to attract Klaus' attention.

"What, you've bought all of this stuff? That must have cost a fortune," is his immediate observation.

I try to placate him by listing all the items I have borrowed: a jacket for Max, gaiters for both of us, a pair of gloves, and a few beanies.

"And look, I'm finally using the 20 jillion hand-warmers you bought," I point out helpfully, in an effort to divert attention from *my* shopping excesses to *his*.

"Well, I never see you putting this much effort into packing when we are traveling together," he grumbles before fleeing the scene of destruction.

And he is right. Never before have I been so diligent in making sure we have absolutely everything we need when we step off that plane. In my defense, never before have I tried to scale a 19,000-plus foot mountain, either.

I take special comfort in dumping an avalanche of hand and toe warmers onto my pile, the ones from the Costco box that so serendipitously traveled to our garage in South Africa. If they put me over the 15 kilogram weight limit, I'm willing to discard anything from my stash to make room. Hairbrush, toothpaste, underwear, fresh socks – you name it. Warm always trumps clean – that's the one thing I've learned from the few occasions I've actually gone camping before.

The next task is organizing and getting it all under control, helped greatly by one of the wonders of modern civilization: the Ziploc bag. There isn't much in life you can't organize into Ziploc bags to instantly feel good about yourself. It's one of America's greatest inventions (it *is* an American invention, isn't it?) and rather hard to come by in South Africa. Not all Ziploc bags are created equal, and I feel lucky to have secured an entire box of original Ziploc brand gallon-sized freezer bags in a recent barter trade.

Nevertheless, I almost despair at the magnitude of the task at hand. It's hard to make a thousand small decisions, to determine whether one or two long-sleeve shirts are needed, for instance, or to figure out where exactly in the bag an item must go. And then, at the last moment, everybody and their brother seems to suddenly have something to say about what should be packed and how and in which bag, so that I end up rearranging everything again and again. Things like "toilet paper not in a roll but in individual sheets in a Ziploc bag" and "gear you'll summit with *not* in the bag you're checking in case it gets lost on the flight."

What? I've spent the better part of last month buying stuff and reading lists and borrowing things all in the name of winnowing down my life so it can fit into a smallish duffel bag, and now there's a chance I will not even have that bag with me when climbing the mountain?

There is nothing to be done but to take that already zippered-up bag of mine I was so proud of moments earlier and totally repack everything once more, separating carry-on and check-in items. You don't want to start your Kili climb without your hiking boots. Or the toilet paper. Or the down sleeping bag. Or pretty much everything else your packing list tells you to bring. Once I've taken everything out of the bag that I'll absolutely positively need for climbing Kili, there's practically nothing left in the original bag. Except for my notebook, the package of dried mangoes, and one spare t-shirt. I take comfort in the fact that these three guys will travel in style, bouncing around with ample space while everything else is now crammed into what I can only hope will pass as a carry-on bag when I get onto the plane.

When I take a breather and sit down with *Across East African Glaciers: An Account of the First Ascent of Kilimanjaro*, I find that once again Hans Meyer, the first man to summit, described it best: "Our preparations, which of course included a thousand details it is impossible to enumerate here, occupied three months." That is exactly how I feel. There were definitely a thousand details, and they also seem to have occupied me for the last three months.

You'd think that 120 years later things would have become a tad easier. And indeed they have. After all, I won't have to carry a mercurial barometer with me to figure out the altitude, I haven't had to special order a pocket chronometer from Dresden, and I certainly haven't been prefilling cartridges with gunpowder to save myself the hassle of filling them each time I want to shoot my gun. Indeed, Meyer's gun collection alone is reason to bless the conveniences of modern times in that I won't have to bring a variety of handguns and small artillery to cover anything from fowl to elephant to rebellious native. I also say a silent prayer to bless the existence of such a place as Trappers, saving me the hassle of having to order my sun-helmet from Mssrs. Silver & Co. in London and galvanized iron oil-cans from F.A. Schulze on the Fehrbelliner Strasse in Berlin. Again, I can't help but feel a bit ashamed that I've been fretting so much over my packing when clearly others before me have managed to overcome much bigger packing challenges.

I do, however, have one special hardship in my column that Herr Meyer can't touch: I'm bringing along a teenager. And of course Max hasn't lifted a finger in the packing department. Instead, he's been busy milking every last ounce of online time out of his computer and battling armies of Russian-sounding villains on the Xbox. Shopping for boots was exactly the kind of battle of wills I had predicted, and since then I have refrained from dragging Max along. Whatever suitable pants and fleeces I found I brought home for fittings and returned if necessary, duly checking a box on my list after each addition and then unchecking it again when a return was necessary – there's nothing worse than unchecking a checked to-do! I've issued a whole host of reminders and countdowns, but as usual, Max's plan has been to throw everything together in ten minutes just before we leave. Oh, the blessings of having a mother to rely on who'll make sure to pack your mittens so that you won't lose any fingers to frostbite, even though you've told her to leave you alone. Once again, I've thrown all advice of "natural consequences" from my parenting self-help shelf to the wind and have packed his bag too.

And now everything is finished. I can't help but feel extremely smug to have fit our whole lives, or at least the next seven days of it, into a bunch of clear plastic bags, right there for everyone to see. And to be done with my packing with two full days to go. That, Klaus can assure you, has never ever happened before.

I think we're ready.

The People We'll be Stuck
With for a Week

I'm sure you cannot wait to have some profound questions answered. Like will or will she not use the garden trowel? And will she win the award for most layers of clothing during summit night? I quite agree. After all these months of preparations, I, too, cannot wait to finally get started. But first, let me introduce you to the main characters of our Kili expedition.

There are ten people in our group so far: four men and three women, all of us more or less in our mid-40s and early 50s, and three 16-year-old boys. The boys have the distinct advantage of a) possessing young legs and especially knees, b) not having expended an ounce of energy on any kind of packing or even thinking about packing up to this point, and c) having gone on a ten-day camping expedition at high altitude in the Drakensberg with their school a few months ago. They even carried their own tents and did their own cooking and therefore don't seem to be terribly impressed with the magnitude of what we're trying to accomplish.

Once we start our climb, of course, we'll see our group vastly expanded. Thirty porters, more or less, will be tasked with carrying all our gear and food, and we'll be led by a guide and several assistants. It still feels totally decadent having so many people cater to our group, but that's the way Kili expeditions have been run from the day they first started, so I'm not going to object.

Quite a few people climbing Kili, I am to find out, embark on their trips solo. They fly into Kilimanjaro airport from wherever they happen to live and then meet whomever they're grouped with for the very first time at their hotel. I imagine that leaves quite a bit of room for pre-departure fretting. Will I be stuck with speed-talker who won't shut up for ten days? Will everyone else be super-fit and leave me behind in the dust? Will one of them be a pessimist who drags the whole group down? I told you I'm not typically one to bother too much with such questions, but nevertheless I'm glad I won't have to because I already know the climbers in our group.

First, we've got Mike, who I've already introduced, and who has been so essential to the early planning of our enterprise. At some point during the course of next week we'll christen him "The Fat Controller" (from the *Thomas the Tank Engine* series). To be fair, he is neither fat nor wears a top hat, but he does love to direct everyone around. On the other hand, Mike is the most adventure-loving person I've ever known. In fact, he is only truly happy when things go wrong. His face will light up when the boat trailer gets stuck in the soft mud, and he will have the time of his life scouring the environs for a piece of old wire that can be fashioned into a pulley. He will try to ford a river in the Okavango Delta just to see if his Toyota truck can handle it without a broken axle and for the pleasure of retelling the story later in great, embellished detail. He can boast two prior Kili climbs, one successful and the other one aborted due to altitude sickness but refashioned into the conquest of nearby Mount Meru, equally tantalizing and no less challenging.

In fact, by all accounts it sounds like Mount Meru is the better mountain in almost every respect. It's far less crowded – in fact positively lonesome – and it's much cleaner as a result; it offers much more in terms of wildlife viewing; it's much cheaper to climb; it poses perhaps more technical challenges to the climber interested in them; it exudes its own thrill of danger in that it last erupted as recently as 1910 (whereas the last major eruption of Kilimanjaro was over 200,000 years ago); you're likely to get some great views of Kilimanjaro from afar; and you run almost no risk of having to abort the mission due to altitude sickness. Oh, and when you're on the summit, you can take a picture next to the sign proclaiming *Socialist Peak*. I'm not even kidding you. And yet all of this has no chance against the words "I climbed Mount Kilimanjaro," and so Mount Meru will forever remain the forgotten one.

Also in our group is Martin, the youngest of the adults as well as the tallest. He's the only one in our party most of us haven't met before. He is a cousin of Mike's and is flying in from Australia where he currently resides, via the United States where he is in the process of moving to. Or vice versa – I don't quite remember. Due to his British origin – the English are endowed with the best sense of humor; it must be in their blood – you can always count on Martin to be ready with a dry joke when it's needed most, and he's also the only one in our group lugging a proper DSLR camera up the mountain. I will be hitting him up for gratuitous pictures for sure.

The next two climbers joined the group as a couple – Dudley and Sharon. Dudley's wit is just as sharp and quick as Martin's, and in fact I seem to recall his origins are also British if you care to go back enough decades, though he is most definitely a South African now. Having Dudley and Martin in our group will ensure that our conversations won't be too boring over the next ten days. I've already mentioned Dudley's partner Sharon, my friend who runs the equestrian therapeutic center. She's the philosopher of sorts in our group, always able to find the deeper meaning, as in her brilliant analysis of "Just give us a mountain" back when we were being pestered by the Spanish Inquisition about our plans. I'm a bit jealous of Sharon because she's the only one who will have a mate with her, and I imagine she'll be spending her nights in a super-toasty double sleeping bag without fear of the cold. Only, considering the nickname we are later to endow Dudley with, maybe my envy about the sleeping bag is a bit premature.

The last of the men in our group is Adrian who admits he's not entirely sure why he signed up for this particular adventure. Being a good sport, he joined our group not so much because he had his reasons for climbing Kili but because he couldn't find one not to. He and his wife Andy are Klaus' and my weekend tennis partners, and while the four of us have distinguished ourselves more with our ability to trash-talk than with any brilliant plays, we have great fun during our occasional Sunday afternoon matches. We have even more fun during the long poolside wine-and-cheese sessions afterwards – the real purpose of our get-togethers. I suspect a wine-tasting trip to South Africa's fabled Cape wine region complete with lavish dinners at award-winning restaurants would be higher up on Adrian's personal ranking of possible vacation activities than hiking up a mountain. In fact, I can't say that I don't agree. Also, I feel a certain kinship with Adrian, because like me he has brought along a teenage son who doesn't like to lift a finger in vain.

That teenage son is David, a classmate and friend of Max's. I suspect Adrian has talked him into the whole thing by advertising the fact that Max is coming, when of course I have employed the very same tactic the other way around. I'm still surprised the two of them didn't wise up and plan a weeklong Xbox marathon at one of our houses while they had the place practically to themselves. Before having even walked one step, I feel quite victorious about that little parenting accomplishment.

Rounding out the female contingent of our little platoon is my dear friend Monia, who, in addition to being my boot camp mate, is also a fellow expat. Originally from Belgium, she is sociable, chatty, and always positive of attitude. She also has a flaming red mane of curly hair. I don't know a more enthusiastic person – about this trip, and about life in general. It's also safe to say she is the most compulsive planner in our group, with a bag packed to the hilt and forever asking questions in her lilting accent. You wouldn't know that she's already climbed Kili, but she has – quite successfully. Just to be safe, she seems to want all her questions answered once again. The disappearing snow is what's luring her to Mount Kilimanjaro a second time. And, who knows, perhaps the fact that this time her husband won't be coming along. He apparently vowed to never ever do summit night again after their first (and his last) Kili climb. Something I try not to ponder.

By the way, I'm a bit intimidated by the physical fitness everyone is bringing along with them. Adrian and David seem to have logged more road and mountain biking miles between the two of them than *Team US Postal Service*, and they have successfully competed in South Africa's two largest cycling races for years. Mike, though he might not look like it, would probably outlast all of us if it ever came to it, driven by pure energy and will. As Jacky will tell you, Mike only runs on two speeds – all out or nothing. Mostly all out, from what I've seen. Monia is the one I can't keep up with during my boot camp runs around the cricket field where she has pushed me to the limits of utter exhaustion, and Sharon is an excellent horsewoman who competes in harness races (I like to think of them as chariots) in her spare time. While I don't know of any sporting accomplishments on Dudley's part, I know that he'll be equipped for anything this mountain might throw at us because he carried not 12 kilograms of brick but more like 15 kilograms of toddler on every single one of our test hikes. Hannah – Sharon and Dudley's beautiful adopted daughter – loved every minute of riding high in daddy's back carrier during our Sunday walks, and I wouldn't be entirely surprised if she somehow showed up at the foot of Kili, beaming at us and holding up her little arms to be lifted in the carrier.

I wonder how easily I'll keep up with all of them. People often ask me if I run a lot, and with the exception of the last few months of boot camp I can honestly say that I've never done any running in my life. At least not something I'd officially call running. Perhaps that is one thing I should be grateful to my four children for. I did have to run after them quite a bit when they were little, and this must have kept me reasonably fit.

The other teenager in the group is Dylan, to whom, as we have learned, we more or less owe the fact that we've arrived at this point, ready to embark on the adventure of our lifetimes. He is the most gung-ho about our climb, competing with Mike, his father, over who can haul more bricks and who is less of a sissy. They also seem to have packed only one fleece between the two of them and are often to be heard fighting over who gets to wear it.

And, finally, there is Max, the third and last of the teenagers. He's known to be stubborn, in fact so stubborn that he's earned the nickname Zax, just like the North- and South-Going Zaxes in Dr. Seuss's *Prairie of Prax*. We were once parked in an icy parking lot in Indiana for hours in one of our standoffs and, just as in the story, we weren't that far away from a bridge being constructed to guide traffic around us. Max says he doesn't like his nickname, but whenever I think I might have to look for a new one, another Zax moment arrives and we're back to square one. But being stubborn also means he is strong-willed, not easily swayed by popular opinion, and one of the greatest debaters I've ever met. And he is by far the most courageous one in our family when it comes to jumping from high places.

I'm hoping he is also well prepared when it comes to climbing to high places.

Getting There

We are all gathered at O.R. Tambo International Airport in Johannesburg, and it's time to say good-bye to those staying behind. In my case, it means saying good-bye to Klaus for a long time as he is heading back to the United States in a few days to start his new assignment, whereas I'm staying behind with the children to finish the school year in South Africa.

It feels strange, because for once saying "I'll call you when I get there" doesn't make much sense. I will mostly be off the grid for the next ten days. I think that sounds more exhilarating to me than to him. For some reason, I like the idea of no one knowing exactly where I'll be.

Because of this new job of his, my Kili adventure almost didn't happen at all. Here we were peacefully cruising along in our South African expat life, full of ideas for more places to travel and explore, when out of the blue he got the call to move on to a new posting in the US. We agonized over what would be the optimal time for the kids to move schools yet again, and whether it might not be best to make the leap right away so they could start the American school year at its beginning, but in the end we decided against it. Which meant the Kili climb was still on for me, except now with the added hurdle of having to find a nanny for the three kids staying behind, since Klaus wouldn't be there with them. In a lucky confluence of events, it just so happened that Julia, a young friend of ours from Germany, had been asking to visit us during her last summer before starting college. We convinced her to book for September, her status was upgraded from visitor to babysitter, and that was that. We are very grateful to Julia and her family for this timely and generous contribution to the Kilimanjaro expedition. The three children couldn't be in any better hands while we are gone.

Once we've said all our good-byes, I'm beginning to look forward to the flight. Not so much because of where it's taking me, but because of who is on it. Or, rather, who is *not* on it. I'm traveling with just thirty-three percent of the usual contingent.

Don't get me wrong, I truly love my family, but traveling with all of them in a group can be a bit, well, exhausting.

It typically starts before we even leave the house. Have you ever tried to go anywhere with six people? It's nearly impossible to leave on time. Every single time we want to leave the house, it's like we're going on a bus tour to Florida with a group of retirees. Building in extra time usually doesn't help, because it just moves the frenzy and the fights and the arguments to an earlier hour. The kids will need to run back into the house to first retrieve an iPod and then a stuffed animal and then a sweatshirt, but the one thing they will not remember during all that running to and fro is that they forgot to flush the toilet, and invariably we're greeted with a very foul smell upon our return two weeks later. When we finally make it to the airport, the check-in procedure beckons. My husband tenses up as soon as we approach the counter, while the kids choose this very moment to tell me their life stories, all four at the same time, and I get so busy answering them all that the bags don't get hustled onto the belt quickly enough, winding the husband up even tighter.

Thank goodness there is the security check to look forward to.

"When will we get there?"

"Are we flying business class?"

"Do we have to go through security?"

I get bombarded with all this on the way to security, yet no one ever ponders the really important questions, like what to put in their backpacks, or, more precisely, what to take out of them and leave at home. We've had to surrender so many scissors at airport security that they could outfit an entire elementary school class in Afghanistan with them. And even odder items have attracted attention, like the light-up bouncy ball one of the girls had stuffed in her backpack after a birthday party. The electronics in it aroused suspicion, and the thing had to undergo an explosives test. Then it had to be shown around to all the security staff – in the same way a patient with a rare disease is paraded before all the hospital interns – before we could finally move on.

On we move to the gate and then the plane. Or wait, not the plane quite yet. There was the time we had been sitting at the gate for over an hour – remember, we almost always get there very early – waiting for the boarding call, and when it finally came, Klaus scanned all our carry-on bags and declared that one was missing. He opened his mouth for what might have become a lengthy tirade about our collective irresponsibility, but I was already huffing and puffing back in the direction of the security check, followed by one of the boys and hoping we'd still find the bag intact rather than destroyed by the bomb squad. We instantly regretted not having dumped our backpacks with their laptops in them before taking off, but there was nothing to be done but keep running until our legs were Jell-O and our lungs about to burst. The bag was eventually found, the boarding agent sweet-talked long enough to delay the closing of the gate, and a big marital blowup was avoided by the skin of our teeth.

At other times we fail to foresee the inevitable squabble over who gets to sit where. There are six people with very specific requirements: one absolutely needs an aisle seat, one must sit next to Mom, a third one must *not* sit next to her brother, and a fourth hasn't gotten the window seat since the French Revolution. It's basically a logistical impossibility to accommodate everyone, which means we usually have to trade concessions now against future promises, lighting up the entire debate again the next time around because of course I can't be trusted to remember who got what for more than five minutes.

Needless to say, once we finally sit in our seats I go straight for the wine and then a refill, trying hard to ignore the apple juice that just got spilled over my lap. Or the retching sounds coming from the seat in front of me, an inescapable reminder that we have, once again, forgotten to load up on anti-motion-sickness pills for son number two.

I've checked and re-checked all the paperwork, making sure I have money and passports, including visas, as well as yellow fever certificates. Usually it's Klaus who holds on to all the travel documents. I'm a bit nervous when this job falls squarely onto me.

I don't think the yellow fever certificates are required, especially when you're flying directly to Kilimanjaro from overseas, but as we already have them from our stay in Zanzibar, I've brought them along. The only time you can be sure not to be asked for a document is when you actually have it on you. But thinking of yellow fever now makes me think of vaccinations in general. Are there any shots Max and I should have gotten? I've been so absorbed in counting out pieces of toilet paper and stuffing my bag with hand warmers, I totally neglected to investigate immunization requirements.

Not that I've neglected the medical checklist. We have Diamox, malaria pills, and a prophylactic package of antibiotics. We have blister bandages, Ibuprofen, Ace wraps, Burnshield, and Tylenol. We have antihistamines, hydrocortisone cream, and Imodium for our bowels. We even have Dramamine to combat nausea, even though I've never heard of anyone getting motion sickness from walking. The only thing we don't have in our first aid kits is "cow lymph" as carried by Hans Meyer in 1889 to vaccinate everyone should there be a smallpox outbreak. But I do now wonder if I shouldn't have paid attention to some other more modern diseases of east Africa.

Of course I'm only thinking of these things when it's too late. I went into a similar state of panic just a few days ago when someone mentioned the word insurance. As in "We made sure the travel insurance policy we got covered evacuations from the mountain." I wanted to strangle them. Neither evacuation nor purchasing insurance for the event had ever entered my mind. The thing is, my panic didn't arise at the thought of Max or myself possibly needing to be evacuated. That I could handle. More accurately, it arose over the realization that *should* Max or I need to be evacuated and the bill henceforth be presented to Klaus, he would probably kill me for having neglected to think ahead. "I can't believe you forgot the travel insurance," might be his words as I am lying in the hospital hooked up to an IV and practically dying. I have reason to fear this. The last time I *was* lying in a hospital bed hooked up to an IV and practically dying, his words just an hour earlier when I couldn't drag myself out of bed on account of a bad bout of the flu had been: "Pull yourself together!" We were in the process of moving countries at the time, and he strongly felt that rather than lying in bed I should busy myself packing up our belongings.

I spent the better part of a day consulting the TIC travel insurance brochure I had dug up from the thicket of Kili emails in my inbox, wondering whether I should get "leisure comprehensive" or "leisure standard," and whether we should rather cover for "war and terrorism" or "hijack, hostage, or wrongful detention." But in the end my panic was unwarranted, as it turned out our existing expat health insurance policy did indeed cover evacuations from wherever we might be stranded and in ill enough health to need evacuation. And Mount Kilimanjaro wasn't listed in any of the exceptions.

A word to the fellow traveler about passports and visas: it's a good idea to obtain the Tanzania visa ahead of time at one of their embassies. I can safely say this because, ahem, I have first-hand experience of not doing it.

When we traveled to Zanzibar about a year ago, it seemed much easier to get our visas upon arrival rather than driving all the way to the embassy in Pretoria. All you had to bring, we were told, was 50 US dollars per person. It sounded easy enough, except when we got there the price was suddenly 100 dollars for those of us with an American passport, versus 50 dollars for the German ones. No one had mentioned a visa discrimination policy depending on your country of citizenship, but there it was, Americans being squeezed at twice the rate of other travelers. We are a family of dual citizens – three of us American-born but also German due to parental lineage, and three of us foreign-born but also American due to recent naturalization – and for some reason this time we had only each brought the passports of our birth country. There we stood in the stuffy arrivals building amidst a throng of perspiring travelers with three passports of each kind and about 50 dollars short (we had brought some extra, just in case, but not enough).

What to do? We had already shifted from one foot to the other in the sweltering heat for a good hour, stuck behind a large corporate group from Hyundai hogging the

visa counter. Half of them were totally drunk after the
four-hour flight from Johannesburg, and you couldn't
really blame them. They had probably been drinking to
suppress the nagging feeling that this was one of those
decrepit African airplanes everyone always vows to never
fly on. Its tattered seats inspired no confidence that the
engines were any better maintained, but we had arrived
safely in Zanzibar, and now Klaus was setting off to find
an ATM while I remained at the visa counter with the
kids, my eyes firmly on the stack of our passports that was
now sitting somewhere behind the glass window.
Occasionally an official would ask me about the missing
50 dollars – I had already given them the 400 we did bring
– and I'd just shake my head and mouth *sorry* through the
glass. Then they'd process somebody else and eventually
turn back to me, asking the same question, at which I'd
shake my head mournfully once more.

In the end we were waved through, not with the
actual visas but just some kind of stamp with scribbled
notes in the margin. That is the beauty of Africa. Someone
must have decided that 400 dollars was a decent haul and
the extra 50 dollars not worth extended effort. Or maybe
they were flabbergasted as to what to do with us, because
we were "white people who seemed to have time on their
hands," in the words of one of my favorite African
authors, Peter Godwin.

You will almost always fare better in Africa if you
have plenty of time.

You would think my Zanzibar visa experience
prepared me well for our Kili trip. It did, inasmuch as I
thought ahead this time – uncharacteristically, some might
say – and made sure to use the German passports for both
Max and myself when getting the visas. Who doesn't like
to save 100 dollars?

My blunder with this line of reasoning doesn't
register until we're already in the air and it's too late.

While my German passport holds my South African visa, which is what we need to get back into the country upon our return, Max has *his* South African visa in his American passport, which I didn't bring. I now have ten days to figure out how to sweet-talk a South African immigration officer into letting Max back in without a visa.

It might help me pass the time while I trudge up the mountain.

Our Kenya Airways flight takes us through Nairobi, which is part annoying – there used to be a direct Johannesburg-Kilimanjaro flight but it was cut some time ago – and part thrilling, as I've never been to Kenya. We pass the time of our layover salivating over the Milka chocolate display in one of the shops and trying to figure out how to convert South African rands to Kenyan shillings, because Milka is one product you won't find on South African grocery shelves, and we're eager to have some. Before we have time to put our calculations to the test, however, we are called to embark on our final leg via Precision Air. It's a good thing too, because I don't think there is a sliver of space to spare in any of our packs, not even for chocolate.

It's a short flight from Nairobi to Kilimanjaro airport, and the highlight is seeing snow-covered Kibo – the highest peak of the Kilimanjaro range – right outside our window as we pass by. The massive cone is magnificent, bathed in a soft rosy glow in the early morning light. We get an even better look at Mount Meru, in itself an impressive mountain. I try not to think about the fact that our small plane has been climbing nonstop from the moment we lifted off, and that Kilimanjaro still seems to loom above rather than below us when we pass by it. It's an enormous mountain, there is no denying it.

And we'll be walking up its slopes a day from now. I'm beginning to grasp what a huge undertaking this will be.

If nothing quite equals *pole pole* in contributing to your success in making it all the way to the summit of Kili, nothing equals *pole pole* in contributing to your impatience early on. From the moment you first arrive at your hotel in Moshi – in our case, the Springlands Hotel, but there are dozens, possibly hundreds, just like it – events move at a *pole pole* pace.

Because our Joburg-Nairobi-Kilimanjaro flight left at such an ungodly hour, we roll into the courtyard of our hotel on Saturday morning and have an entire day at our disposal. We are shown to our rooms – basic but with all the necessities, especially the mosquito nets – and we try to catch a glimpse of Mount Kilimanjaro by leaning out the window and craning our necks in what we think is the right direction, but all we see is a thick layer of clouds. Then we rummage through our belongings – which we are grateful to note have all arrived – and get them into the order we think is best for the coming week. We pack and repack our bags, we rent hiking poles from the hotel store (definitely useful!), we buy a few bottles of water to supplement the ones we've already packed, and we take a long shower while we still have access to one.

When there's absolutely nothing left to do, the waiting begins. We sit around for quite some time until a guy shows up to give us a briefing, which turns out to be a complete waste of time because we learn nothing we need to know. It's the most boring briefing ever, delivered in a monotone by a guy we are happy to learn will *not* be our guide. It would be torture to be stuck on a mountain with him and his wheezy voice for a week.

What we *do* need to know we find out from some kindly South Africans who have just returned that very morning from their climb and are thrilled to hear that apparently we've been assigned to the same guide they have come to love over the previous seven days.

Think about this for a moment: our guide and his team have just returned from summiting Kili, and tomorrow they'll turn around and do the same thing again, on only one night's rest. Remarkable.

Equally remarkable are their names. Our head guide is Godlisten, Goddy for short. His name in Swahili is Mungu Sikiliza, which I'm not sure how to pronounce, so I think we'll have to stay with Goddy. Our assistant guide is Hillary. We christen him Sir Edmund on the spot and cannot help but feel confident that such auspicious names will have to lead to success.

We notice something else about this South African group. They look energized, positively radiant. Haven't they just put the most grueling exercise behind them? Don't they want to collapse onto their beds? But instead they are out here in the courtyard, bubbling over in their excitement to share their experience. I can't help but wonder if that'll be us a week from now, and how exactly it will feel.

But for the moment, we have more pressing business. The question we are dying to have answered is the one about the toilet situation. Up until this point I have successfully suppressed all thoughts about this, figuring there is nothing to be done about it.

But it turns out there is, and it doesn't involve the use of the garden trowel from my packing list.

"You *must* get the toilet tent," chirps the tanned woman in a pretty sundress.

A private toilet tent? I had no idea there is such a thing. "Can't we just use those drop toilets?"

I throw this out mainly to make conversation, as we have all the time in the world and Briefing Guy is still droning on in the background.

She looks at me in horror.

"Just hire the porter with the toilet tent. Trust me!"

By the way, if you're not enjoying the toilet talk, you
might as well skip the next couple of chapters. Hiking on
Kilimanjaro – or any other mountain, I presume – reduces
your topics of interest to three things: when will I eat,
where will I sleep, and where do I shit, excuse my
language. And not only will *you* be preoccupied with this.
Everyone else in your group will be more in tune with
your bodily functions than you ever wished for. Part of
this is fueled by boredom and taking an interest in your
fellow man to an extent you wouldn't under normal
conditions, and part of it is fueled by strategy. ("I tried my
best to get in there ahead of major infiltration by others in
our party" is the confession of one veteran Kili climber
when asked about the toilet tent.)

Just know that it could be worse. I could have written
an entire how-to guide about "what to do in nature when
nature calls." And what to do with the, ahem, results. I've
glanced at a book with the glorious title of *How to Shit in
the Woods* – yes, that's what it's called, I'm not even
shitting you – and was particularly captivated by the
chapters entitled "Anatomy of a Crap" and "How Not to
Pee in Your Boots." But I hesitated at "Group Shitarees" –
what the hell are those? – and came to a dead stop at
"Becoming a Poop Packer." I don't want to know anything
about how poop and packing ended up in the same
sentence – ever. It makes the garden trowel look positively
inviting.

In any case, a private toilet tent is apparently just that
– a little tent with enough room for a bucket topped with a
toilet seat that gives you complete privacy from prying
eyes. Not so much from prying ears, alas, but still
infinitely better than having to use the infamous drop
toilets all the camps are outfitted with. If you're planning
to frequent *those* toilets, you might as well not worry about
altitude sickness, because there is no doubt you'll be

fainting from the smell way before you've even reached 3,000 meters.

So I'm asking you: What would you be willing to spend for the luxury of someone carrying this private toilet tent up the mountain for you and cleaning it out and making it presentable in every camp so that you only have to share it with nine other people rather than three hundred?

I'm guessing a lot more than 10 US dollars per person. Yes, that is possibly the best bargain of any kind I have ever come across.

I mention three hundred people. If you've been under the illusion that climbing Kilimanjaro is for nature lovers or anyone seeking the solitude of the great outdoors, you might think again. Somewhere between 25,000 to 35,000 climbers attempt to summit every year, from what I've meticulously researched online.

Okay, I Googled it and went with the first link.

Anyway, just think about that number for a moment. It's not even all that much when you compare it to other tourist sites around the world. The Louvre gets approximately that many visitors in one *day*, and even more flock to Niagara Falls. And yet, if you do the math, this puts the number of people on the mountain in any given week at between 500 and 700, and certainly much higher during peak season, which of course is the season we picked for our climb. So my guess of about 300 people in camp on any given day in September is probably not too far off. Which means each night you set up camp amidst a buzzing tent city, all of them spaced just a few meters apart, a distance allowing for a lot of nocturnal noise sharing, if you must know the truth. Whichever of the six official routes up the mountainside you choose, it will often resemble a busy highway more than a hiking trail, particularly as everyone gets closer to the summit. You're much more likely to step on someone else's toes –

and, frankly, someone else's turds – than see any wildlife or enjoy a moment of solitude.

It's a beehive.

But it doesn't matter. Everyone has come for the same purpose, and you all share one big goal: standing on Uhuru Peak on Day Six, at 5,895 meters, long enough to snap the group picture so you can get the hell out of there again as fast as your legs will carry you.

Godlisten and Hillary

PART II – THE CLIMBING

"Haba na haba, hujaza kibaba" (Little by little, fills the pot).

– Swahili proverb

Day One: Pole Pole

Machame Gate to Machame Hut, Sunday Sep 2, 2012
Distance: 9-10 km, 5-7 hours
Elevation: 1,200 m climb from 1,800 m to 3,000 m

The big day has finally arrived. It starts punctually, but *pole pole*. *Pole pole* starts before we even get to the park gate, because just minutes into our bus ride we stop on some side street in Moshi "to get a few things." I idly gaze out at the shops around us, and a gruesome cow carcass dangling in one of the windows is staring right back at me. I wonder if the cow is one of the "things" we are getting but push the thought out of my mind. A lively debate has sprung up on the other side where some street vendors are hawking Kilimanjaro bracelets and other trinkets through our open windows.

"You buy, only ten thousand shilling!" one guy urges, only to be shoved away by another guy angling for the sale. It sounds expensive, even though we have no idea what the exchange rate is, and a hotly contested barter begins.

Let me just say that I'm not good at bartering. Or at saying no, for that matter, which can be an expensive combination. My last bartering match made me the proud owner of two ill-fitting cowboy hats that I had absolutely no use for. I briefly considered bringing them along on this trip where they might actually serve a purpose but had the suspicion that they belonged in the zip-off pants category in terms of the coolness factor. So as not to set off Max's teenage embarrassment radar, and also because the hats looked like they might not survive a rainfall, I left them at home.

I prudently refrain from bartering with the vendors outside our bus, but Dylan has no such inhibitions. He asks to see the wares, he negotiates with skillful flair, and a few colorful bracelets change hands for what seems like a decent deal for all sides. I for my part am glad to have escaped the scrutiny of the vendors, or I might have climbed Kili adorned like a Christmas tree.

When Godlisten and Hillary are finished with their errand, they hop back on the bus, and we settle into our bumpy ride.

Once arrived at the park gate, time slows down to an even more *pole pole* pace, if that's possible. We step off the bus and are beckoned into a little hut where we write our names, our ages, and – curiously – our professions into some kind of register. We visit a real toilet for the last time, and then there is nothing left to do but wait.

And wait.

Some of us pass the time by snacking on the lunch packs we've been given, even though it's still morning. That much less to carry up the mountain, is what I'm thinking. Perhaps I also hope it might sufficiently spur my digestive system to warrant another trip to the nice toilet facilities while I have the chance.

Others are happy to have this break to undertake the first repairs. Before we've even taken a single step, David has already managed to lose the bottom piece of his hiking pole somewhere between the hotel and the park gate, and now it is distinctly too short to be of any use. Leave it to Adrian, our engineer, to come up with a solution: the forest supplies a nice piece of wood, an old discarded rubber stopper for the bottom is found among the debris on the path, and with a few skillful flourishes of the

Leatherman tool a refurbished hiking stick is fashioned, good as new and with a lot of character.

By now we've already read and re-read the big signs telling us that we're about to embark on the Machame Route and better heed all the "points to remember," such as making sure we're physically fit, not stricken with a cold or even a sore throat of any kind, and at least ten years of age. We've taken pictures of the monkeys frolicking on top of those signs, and I cannot help but detect a note of mockery in their gaze. "How stupid must you people be to leave the comforts of this place where life is so easy and convenient," they seem to say. We've already shaken our fists at those same monkeys who've made off with the cashews from our lunch packs.

To pass the time, I amble over to where our guide is meeting with the porters he's assembled for the trip. Godlisten, whom we've so far only talked to briefly, seems to be in his element, surrounded by a group of young men in various states of disheveled dress. He is directing everyone, negotiating, speaking rapidly, and making quick decisions. From what I can observe, without speaking any Swahili, I get the impression that he is a master of his trade. Of this I am glad. When he was first introduced to us, I was briefly taken aback. He didn't strike me as the image of fitness, as someone who spends most of his life walking – and most of that up and down steep hills. Hillary, young and strapping in his tight long-sleeve shirt, better fits my idea of what a mountain guide should look like. But Goddy looks to be older than average, is round-faced, and has a decidedly middle-aged paunch around his midsection. Which I suppose just goes to show that you should never judge anyone by their looks.

The place is buzzing with activity this morning, and I'm sure it's like this almost every day of the year. It resembles a busy marketplace, and in a way it is just that.

It is here where all the supplies are divvied up and weighed so that everyone carries about the same load.

A staggering load.

Each of us has a duffel bag allowance of 15 kilograms, which I'm proud to say both Max and I have stayed under by 5 kilograms each. And that's a good thing, because I think Monia with her many layers has gone over the limit, judging by her about-to-burst bag.

Then there are all the tents, plates, cups, chairs, stoves, tables, buckets, and food supplies for seven days. It's a lot of stuff, and it's all laid out here at the park gate in a giant heap, down to the tightly bound bunch of parsley. Struck by a sudden thought, I take a closer look at all the gear. I want to get a sneak peek at the infamous toilet, the one we talked about all day yesterday. If you can believe it, there was quite a debate whether we should indulge in the added luxury of a private toilet and fork over the collective 100 dollars. Especially Mike, forever conscious of keeping up his *I'm-no-sissy* credentials, seemed opposed to the idea. He thought the girls – Monia, Sharon, and myself – were being wussies again. That's one of his favorite terms. And what he pictured when we had this conversation, he has since then confided in me, was a porter with a porcelain toilet on his head climbing up a rock face. This image hasn't ceased to make me chuckle whenever it pops into my head, and I now find my gaze drifting over all the assembled equipment, subconsciously looking for a white toilet bowl. But of course I find nothing of the sort. Our toilet tent seems to be an inconspicuous load.

We get three porters per person, meaning we have an entourage of 30 porters catering to our welfare on the mountain. Thirty-one, to be precise – I forgot toilet man, who by the way is truly overjoyed to have a job for the week, so Goddy tells us. Without our toilet, he'd be staying home without an income.

Each of these porters easily carries 22 kilograms on his shoulders or on his head, and he lugs it all up in half the time it takes you to cover the same distance with your puny daypack. When he gets to that day's camp, his first job is to grab a bucket and make the half-hour hike back down to the next riverbed to fetch the water needed to sustain everybody. Then he helps pitch the tents, cut vegetables, and set the table. And after all that he still finds inspiration to carve *hakuna matata* into the watermelon half that holds the fruit salad, making you laugh out loud while you have dessert.

These are some amazing people.

Finally, close to noon, we set off up the mountain. Disappointingly, the wide path leading into the rain forest looks and feels like a road. A surprisingly steep road, but even so the pace is much slower than you'd prefer. You struggle to find a good rhythm, one foot in front of the other. You lift up your foot for a step, but the person in front of you is moving so slowly, because your guide upfront is moving so slowly, that you cannot in fact put your foot back down yet, making you hover on the spot, leg suspended in midair, and struggling not to topple backwards. As I expected and yet failed to envision, the pace is excruciatingly slow. So this is *pole pole*!

We stop every ten minutes or so to let some porters through who greet us with a friendly *jambo* and a wave as they hurry past us not *pole pole* at all. Why do they get to do that, I wonder? Don't they also have to acclimatize slowly?

Maybe the difference is weed. The South Africans call it *dagga* or *ganja*. We come across some porters who are taking a break and are smoking, and the smell of cannabis is overpowering. Of course I should mention here that I have no clue what that smell is, but the three 16 year olds in our group waste no time informing us with absolute certainty that the sweet scent wafting through the air is that of pot. How they know this, I do not ask. Rather, I'm preoccupied with the thought of how to source some for myself, if this is what makes these guys sprint uphill like mountain goats and disregard *pole pole* altogether.

But, alas, no hawkers are present who might sell us some illicit drugs, and so we continue our slow and rather tedious march up the mountain without them. I have all the time in the world to let my mind wander. Where it wanders is to our most recent hike as a family. This was also in Africa, during a long weekend in June, when South Africans celebrate Youth Day in commemoration of the Soweto uprising of 1976. We took not just our family but two additional teenage boys – who were visiting from Germany – to the town of Wilderness along South Africa's picturesque Garden Route, where we engaged in a weekend filled with the kind of adventures teenage boys thrive on: ziplining, bungee-jumping, and whale watching. But these are also the kind of adventures that weigh heavily on your pocketbook, so on the fourth day we decided it was time for simpler and cheaper entertainment: a hike up the mountain.

Not a mountain, really, but more a hill. Right above Wilderness, next to a meadow where paragliders take off from, there is a place called "Map of Africa." I had no idea what that "Map of Africa" was about, but it sounded promising. And there had to be a magnificent view from up high.

The entire way up the hill I got an earful of complaints from the usual suspects.

"Why do we have to do this?"

"This is the worst idea anyone could ever come up with!"

"Moooooom, I'm tired!"

And, my favorite, "Why can't we be normal like other families? No one else has to walk on a road dodging cars!"

I find it interesting that no one ever mentions normal families when we do fun stuff, like riding four-wheelers through Namibian dunes. I'm sure a lot of "normal" families don't do that, either.

But I had to concede the point about the cars. When planning our walk, I hadn't considered how steep it would be, and that the road was a veritable race track for cars barreling downhill at top speed. It was less mountain idyll and more Nascar than I had pictured.

About halfway up the hill we happened upon a pasture with a few horses. The distraction of petting and feeding them kept open rebellion at bay for a while. But then our path took us straight through a decrepit township, which was when even Klaus began to show signs of mutiny, openly grumbling about my lack of wisdom when planning the hike. I refrained from pointing out that he was the one who insisted that we take a hike in the first place instead of sitting on the beach with a book – something I can do for days at a time.

Our little procession trudging through the dusty township attracted quite a few stares – curious, perhaps, but to us they felt hostile – from the local boys kicking a makeshift ball along the dirt road and the women carrying water buckets on their heads.

White people don't normally walk through a township.

Indeed, white people don't normally walk, period, as our children didn't hesitate to point out repeatedly along the way.

If I've learned one thing as a mother, and a wife, it is to remain cheerful during occasions such as these. So if you picture a woman purposefully striding up a mountain, full of an energy she doesn't necessarily feel, singing full-force and followed by a troop of grouchy kids with murderous looks on their faces who are only keeping up because of their very strong need to remain within earshot so as to better unload all their bickering and sulking, you get a good idea of what that family hike of ours looked like. I made a happy face, even though I could feel a blister forming on my foot. I was striding up the mountain without socks, you see, bare feet chafing in my tennis shoes, because I had ceded my socks to Max at the outset. He had tried not being able to locate his own as a ploy to disqualify him from the hike, but I had totally foiled this cunning scheme by stripping my feet of my socks and handing them over triumphantly.

On and on it went, through the township and past a decrepit corner store with an ancient Coca-Cola sign dangling from the wall, until we finally stood in front of the "Map of Africa," which turned out to be a birds-eye view of a river carving its path in the shape of the southern tip of Africa. Pretty, yes, but just as easily reached by car, as evidenced by the large adjacent parking lot which stood empty. The paragliders were absent that day, so even the excitement by proxy when watching other people's adventures was not to be.

All we saw on that hill was a big grasshopper.

I had to endure a lot of grumbling that day, even more than the dosage most mothers endure on a daily basis, but who knows – maybe I planted a tiny seed in someone, a seed which might come to fruition 20 years from now when my kids might create forced family outings of their own in hopes of strengthening family bonds. If you look to be praised for your work or want to see immediate results, you should never become a parent. Parenting is all about realistic expectations and delayed (perhaps by decades) gratification.

In hindsight, I consider it a miracle that we managed to make everybody walk up that hill in the first place.

I bring my thoughts back to the present and am immensely grateful not to be followed by seven complaining people. This is why I'm so exhilarated to be here: if there's any complaining to be done, I have the luxury of doing it myself. But not now – I reckon I better save my complaints budget for summit night.

The road has narrowed to a path and has become even steeper. There are no cars of course, but there is a lot of traffic nonetheless. The porters are not even walking but jogging (and still never fail to toss a friendly *jambo* our way), trailing a faint scent of cannabis behind them. You have to step to the side every few minutes to let them through.

Just as long as you don't step *too far* to the side, we quickly learn. Or at least carefully watch the ground you're stepping on. A lot of human traffic results in a lot of human waste, I conclude, bringing back all my potty images from before in an entirely new light. The toilet situation on Kili is not just a matter of where you step *out* to do your business. It's a matter of what you step *on*.

The whole excursion so far feels less like a mountain climb and more like the charity run I once participated in (and which I didn't exactly volunteer for). It was one of those actions that classes of elementary school kids enthusiastically sign up for, condemning their slightly less enthusiastic parents to trudge through windy streets on dreary November days holding hands with their offspring while dreaming about the steaming cappuccino they could be sipping instead. It is the same here: there was all that waiting at the start, the crowds of people milling about and stepping on each other's toes, and all the candy wrappers and juice box straws littered around us. The only thing missing to complete the picture is a bib on everyone with a starting number as well as a goody bag full of useless trinkets and coupons for pedicures.

Despite the commotion, every once in a while we come upon an empty stretch of path, and it offers us an opportunity to take in the magnitude and density of the rainforest. Everything is bathed in a soft, misty light, filtering from far above through the canopy. Huge ferns evoke prehistoric times, and the tree trunks are covered in thick ivy and moss. The forest is so green and fertile and seems so full of life, yet is so utterly soundless. It's all a bit eerie and magical.

Until we step around the next bend and stumble onto the group in front of us setting up for their first break. I snap out of my reverie thinking *No shit!* The contrast is staggering. A long table has been set up in the middle of a clearing and covered with a linen table cloth. On it are ten neatly arranged place settings from the finest china, not unlike the kind a young bride's wedding trousseau might have been filled with in the olden days, framed by complete sets of cutlery lined up in perfect symmetry, everything waiting for the dinner guests to arrive. It's as if we've chanced upon an impending picnic at Downton Abbey and the butler Carson has just left after ascertaining all the measurements with his ruler. Or like we've come across the cottage of the Three Bears and are encouraged to sit down and taste from each little bowl using every little spoon. And exactly like in that story, the place settings are not meant for us. We watch, not so much with envy but a certain amount of bafflement, as those other guys sit down to their gourmet meal and are waited on by the staff.

It appears that we've overlooked the "Out of Africa"-themed variant of a Kili climb when planning our trip. But we're not upset. We enjoy the luxury of someone else carrying our luggage and cooking our meals – as I've said before, where else but in Africa can you expect to be totally spoiled when going into the wilderness for a week of roughing it? – but this gourmet meal in the wilderness seems a little over the top. It does remind us, however, of our own lunch packs, which unfortunately are mostly gone, either devoured out of sheer boredom during the long wait this morning or nibbled on along the way.

Because we have no food, and because we don't want to watch others while they eat, we pass through the clearing and continue our march. We are swallowed up by the dark forest once more, and doggedly we press onwards. The eerie silence is a bit disquieting, and much like in a church we only speak in whispers, if at all. Everyone seems to be lost in their own thoughts. I realize that I haven't seen Max since he was goofing around with David and Dylan at the park gate. I imagine it might be like this the entire week. After all, I'm not in charge of the kitchen here, and his search for something to eat is often the only motivation for Max to leave the sanctuary of his room and grace the rest of the family with his presence. That's the irony about raising kids: For years they run between your legs and pester you with questions all day long, leaving you to wish for nothing more than a moment of peace and quiet. And then, once they've grown into young adults and when you might actually want to have a conversation with them, when you think it should be your turn to ask some questions, they want nothing to do with you any longer.

After almost seven hours of walking we glimpse the camp not far in front of us. I admit that I'm relieved to be here. Throughout the afternoon the path has been so steep that it mostly consisted of huge steps, cut into the slope and reinforced with wooden planks so that it felt like we were climbing up a giant and endless staircase. Each upward stride was so strenuous that we walked *pole pole* on our own accord and without any admonishments by the guides. No one seemed to have the urge to move any faster, not even the three boys. The reward for our hard work is that we have conquered an astonishing 1,200 meters of elevation in just one day, going from the park gate at 1,800 m above sea level – an elevation already a bit higher than Johannesburg at 1,600 m – all the way to Machame Hut at 3,000 m.

And here, in front of the hut, we are greeted with a welcome sight: Our tents are already waiting for us, ready to be occupied. Except now a slight organizational snag becomes apparent, in that we do not seem to have enough tents among us. Two in our group have signed up for single tents, and yet there are only five tents available for ten people. The obvious solution is to have the two people in single tents – Monia and Martin – team up to share a tent, and Mike immediately appropriates this as his new mission. He's done a lot of camping in the bush, and he seems to be a fan of sharing tents with virtual strangers.

"Come on, look at Martin here," he says to Monia with a twinkle in his eye. "Such a handsome lad! It'll be fun!"

And on he goes, taking turns to describe each of them in more and more glowing terms as a potential tent mate for the other. Martin, utterly exhausted, is too weak to protest, but Monia becomes more horrified with every new embellishment and is very grateful when Goddy presents an alternate solution. It's actually a bit strange: one moment the tent was missing, and the next it seems to have magically reappeared. This leaves Mike rather disappointed. I have the feeling he enjoys provoking Monia with his lewd jokes, and she always seems to oblige, wandering into his trap like a lamb led to slaughter.

After we've moved into our tents and unpacked our few belongings, we are asked to file into Machame Hut to sign our names and professions into the book again – a procedure we are to repeat every night of our climb. After that we are treated to a wonderful dinner in our very own mess tent, overlooking the sea of clouds below. Incredibly, we have already left the rainforest behind us and are camped under the branches of a few smaller trees.

A meal has never tasted better to me, even though our tableware was definitely never destined for any bride's trousseau. Also, one of the folding chairs is dangerously wobbly, and a nightly game of musical chairs ensues as everyone clamors to avoid it. But the food is good, and plentiful: a big pot of soup, followed by some chicken with potatoes or rice, and a dessert. And always popcorn, nuts, tea, and coffee to our hearts' content.

If the food is good, the company is even better. We have a grand old time recounting the day's happenings and peppering Goddy with questions of things to come. We reflect on the fact that we've hiked through gloomy rainforest all day, barely ever catching a glimpse of the sun, surrounded by those eerie trees and gigantic ferns, and how unusual it is that we didn't get rained on once. Even the road we hiked on first, and later the narrow path, were bone dry. I for one thank our good fortune, as I'm quite happy to never find out if the ponchos I bought are indeed waterproof. Maybe picking early September, one of the dry seasons on the mountain, was in fact a good move.

The other good news is, thanks to a combination of pure luck, the layering of socks (thin ones for underneath, and the thick cushy ones for my second layer), and diligently having worn my boots for the last three months (although most often while sitting at my computer), I have no blisters whatsoever.

Bedtime comes early when you're on the mountain. Mainly because there is only so long you can linger in a mess tent on slanting chairs (and without alcohol), and also because the warmth of your sleeping bag is beckoning. Max and I try to get comfortable in the confines of our tent, and I ask him about his day. "Good," he says cheerfully, turns over, and is sound asleep before I can say anything else. I'm glad that he seems happy. I talked him into this hike, after all, and there was a possibility that he wouldn't like it and – God forbid – announce that he's turning around after a day. On the other hand, I can already tell that I will have to pull each and every word out of him if I want to find out more about what is going through his head while we live through our adventure.

Since it is only 8:00 PM I don my headlamp and try to read a bit. I brought a book because a friend and previous hiker recommended one to ward off sleeplessness. But it doesn't take long for my arms to get too cold. I try reading *inside* my sleeping bag, but that doesn't work either, since there isn't enough space to extend my arms to the distance needed for people my age, and no one has thought to put *"(1) Reading glasses"* on the packing list. After a while I give up, turn off the lamp, and close my eyes.

The downside of turning off your headlamp so early is that this makes for a very long night. Just as I feared, I wake up in the middle of the night and can't go back to sleep. What's more, I feel the first faint stirrings in my bladder. I crawl out of the tent and look around to locate the toilet tent, which I've privately christened *Tee-Tee the Toilet Tent*. What, do you think, are the chances Tee-Tee will be occupied?

Very high, it turns out. It's a veritable zoo out there in front of our green toilet tent where several group members have lined up and are patiently waiting their turn. I shiver from the cold and try to pass the time by staring up the mountain, not wanting to engage in conversation because all I really want to do is snuggle back into my sleeping bag and go to sleep.

And then I'm glad I got up, even if it means I had to unzip and re-zip 15 closures in the process. Because the sight is incredible: Kibo – the Kili peak we're trying to scale, shrouded in clouds and hidden from view all day long – is suddenly towering above us in all its majestic beauty. I can see its snow-covered ridges far above under a moonlit sky, and it looks both foreboding and magnificent. I can also make out tiny lights reflecting off the snow somewhere way up there. At first this puzzles me, but then reality hits me with full force: those lights are other hikers summiting right now in a long line of headlamps.

By the grace of God, that will be us in five days.

Hiking through the rainforest

Day Two: Eggs for Breakfast and Diamox before Lunch

Machame Hut to Shira Plateau, Monday Sep 3, 2012
Distance: 10 km, 5-7 hours
Elevation: 840 m climb from 3,000 m to 3,840 m

Wake-up time is 7:15 AM, with the sun still hiding behind the mountain, and we are greeted with bowls of hot water to start the day. What luxury! We wash and file into the mess tent, the need for which wasn't quite so apparent the previous day when it was nice and warm, but in the chilly morning it provides welcome shelter.

We're not entirely surprised that omelets are on the menu, because we saw Hillary tote a bag of eggs up the mountain yesterday. He was nonchalantly swinging it by his side as if he were coming from the convenience store around the corner. What is surprising, though, is that we are to have eggs for breakfast every single day of our hike. What lengths to go to in order to ensure that we have every possible comfort on the mountain.

And yet, apparently not everyone is so grateful.

"Some people, they are not nice," Goddy tells us. "They always complain about the food."

He has stories about a group that sent the bowl of rice "back to the kitchen," asking for potatoes instead. We find this wildly amusing, and pass the time embroidering this scenario with ever more colorful dialogue.

'...And please bring the caviar after the canapés.'

'I'll have the sushi today, not the soup.'

'We'll take the sherry in the library together with the cigars, thank you very much.'

Then I get mad at these unknown people. What the hell kitchen are they talking about? Do they think there is a mountainside restaurant next door where the food magically appears from? Are they not aware that these cooks are going out of their way to provide a home-cooked meal using less-than-stellar equipment, getting up at the crack of dawn to start boiling water, then feed you, then do the dishes, then race up the mountain carrying your rice (or potatoes, whichever it may be) and everything else on their very backs to get there just in time to start all over again?

Or maybe I just signed up for the wrong tour. Maybe there is the five-star version including a succession of gourmet restaurants that I somehow failed to take note of.

Just thinking about all the effort surrounding our daily feeding makes me ashamed of ever having complained about the hassles of cooking for my family. (Although not entirely. It *is* a hassle to cook for my family.) I would have eaten anything they served us on the mountain, but as it turns out, the food is delicious. And always exactly what is needed to replenish our exhausted bodies. The only thing I will probably not want to eat for a while – maybe like three years – is any more peanuts.

What annoys me most about the "back to the kitchen" story is that this previous group probably never appreciated how accommodating Godlisten and his crew truly are. He says there were complaints to his company after that trip, when in fact he did provide the potatoes that day, as demanded. He tapped into supplies pegged for a future dinner and sent a porter back down the mountain to purchase more. All that hiking just to satisfy one offhand remark from a royal jerk.

We resolve to make sure we voice ample praise to the tour operator when we return, because we have our own story to tell. It concerns the missing tent and how all of a sudden there was an extra one. It is only now that we find out how Goddy solved the problem. We have finished our breakfast and are lingering in our seats for a bit when Hillary emerges through a flap partitioning off the mess tent, still in his striped long johns and coming to tell us the plan for the day. We catch a glimpse into this other "room" we didn't even know existed, and it is impossibly crowded in there, full of gear and bodies. I don't know who all is sleeping in that tight space, but I know with a sudden clarity that Goddy and Hillary, as the two lead guides, were not supposed to be in there; they had planned to use the extra tent for themselves. When the packing mishap became apparent last night, they did not hesitate one second to give up this substantial perk, all in the name of customer satisfaction.

After breakfast it's time to pack our belongings and get on with the other morning ritual: replenishing our water supplies. If *pole pole* is the one admonishment you hear from your guides all day long, the other is *drink!* However much you think you should be drinking, it's never enough. You need to drink even more. Our guides recommend three to four liters per person and it's always a challenge to finish all that. You essentially need to be drinking all the time. I'm glad that in addition to our four water bottles – two for Max and two for me – I also bought water bladders for each of us. We've stuffed them into our backpacks which have a special pocket for just that purpose, and this allows us to sip water more or less continually as we walk.

Each morning's ritual is to distribute all the water into the correct vessels and to add purification tablets as needed. They say the water is boiled, and I'm sure it is, but you can't be certain it was long enough to kill all the bacteria. (Judging by the crowds often behaving in less-than-sanitary ways, there are a lot of bacteria to go around on this mountain.) The chlorination tablets taste awful, like drinking directly from a swimming pool, but you get used to it. Some people recommend iodine drops instead of chlorination tablets. Our group is almost evenly divided into fans of chlorination tablets and fans of iodine drops. There are also water filters one could use and even some kind of pen you hold into a water bottle to somehow zap the bacteria with ultraviolet light, but no one has brought any of those. Probably because they cost a fortune. My chlorination tablets might taste awful, but they were cheap.

Admittedly, my water sanitation research was confined to the following email trail, helpfully started by Mike early on:

Mike: "*I experimented with two methods of water purification today, Iodine and Sodium Dichloroisocyanurate (SD) tablets. The iodine treated water tasted crap. The SD tablets tasted less crap – like drinking pool water. I researched these tablets and found that they are recommended by the World Health Organization (WHO) for the treatment of drinking water. Regards, Mike.*"

To which came Dudley's prompt reply: "*Thanks Mike, One question, how do you know the water tasted like crap? Regards, Dudley.*"

And so it went back and forth. All of a sudden everyone had something to say about the alleged taste of shit. Monia, who at that point was not yet friends with the other climbers in our group, became increasingly alarmed by all our trash talking. I'm sure she was wondering if she might have made a mistake by signing up to join our crazy gang.

In any event, I went for "less crap" and that is exactly how it tastes. Dudley, apparently not trusting Mike's ranking of shades of crap, or perhaps just in an act of open rebellion, went for the iodine drops and now totally swears by them.

Whichever you opt for, tablets or drops, they both have a taste you want to mask. The best way to achieve this is to bring plenty of *Game* or some other energy drink powder, which has the added benefit of rehydrating your body better than water alone. Although I can tell you right now that you'll grow thoroughly tired of *that* taste too. Maybe there is something to that Coca-Cola Route after all.

Many people climb Kili without worrying about water purification and are absolutely fine. In fact, you do have to assume that all water is boiled long enough by the porters, since it is also used in preparing your food. Every Kili menu seems to contain a lot of soup and tea, and short of dropping a purification tablet into each individual bowl you consume, you'd better make peace with the quality of the water. Still, I prefer to put a chlorination tablet into each of our water bottles every morning, just to make absolutely sure. And I also make sure we use that same bottled water to brush our teeth – it would be awful to contend with swimming pool drinking water all week and still pick up giardia just because we've rinsed the toothbrush in the wrong bowl.

There is another unexpected benefit to bringing water purification tablets. Yes, you guessed it – it gives us a new topic to talk about! We happily interrupt our regular broadcasting to discuss the various tastes of all the different tablets and powders and drops we have brought, making sure we pause every few minutes to take a sip from our water hoses while trying not to cringe at the taste. Nothing quite helps you bond with people like shared misery.

It's almost a pity we have to leave camp just as the sun is emerging over the crest, radiating much-welcome warmth. But we have a long day ahead of us. Going from Machame Hut to Shira Plateau is another 10 kilometer hike, with only slightly less gain in elevation than yesterday. We start out at a fairly steep climb, and I'm glad to be using my hiking sticks for the first time, which I let the porters carry together with my duffel bag yesterday. I quickly become a convert to the hiking pole cause, even though I've never used them in my life (and even though I admit that I've smiled condescendingly when I've come across hikers with poles in the past), as they take some weight off your weary legs. Not so much off your weary arms and shoulders, however, which begin to tell you promptly at 1:00 PM each day that they've done enough hiking.

Even though the net elevation will be less than yesterday, it's too early to celebrate. It would be fine if all you did was go up, but it soon becomes apparent that we will have to go up and down again to get there. If you check out the map for the Machame Route and look at the side-view profile, you will see that there are quite a few peaks and valleys (whereas the Marangu or Coca-Cola Route goes uphill at a very steady clip). This "up" and "down" has the distinct advantage that it enables you to climb high and sleep low when hiking this route, one of the most important tools to help acclimatize your body to the elevation.

The constant up and down is just not such a great tool to acclimatize your *mind* to the task at hand. Within minutes, what you have so painfully labored up for hours is gone, poof, kaput. All that work, just to do it again the next day, and the next, and the one after that. Of course we end up gaining a bit of elevation each time, but not nearly as much as the long daily marches would suggest.

I've fallen into such a monotonous trot that I've failed to notice the natural beauty all around us, and only when I look up from the path for the first time do I take note of the change in scenery. The evergreen forest has gotten sparser and the growth of the trees more stunted, and the soft forest floor has given way to hardened red dirt, deeply ridged where water has cascaded down the mountain. We are walking amidst a blooming sea of gorgeous daisy-like flowers of the genus *Helichrysum*, which commonly occurs in southern Africa. Some of these flowers – members of the sunflower family – retain their colors particularly well and are therefore well-suited for bouquets of dried flowers, which might explain why they look so familiar. Except that this species, *Helichrysum kilimanjari*, is white as snow, and the flowers we see around us are gathered in large white fields on the gently rising slopes, much like patches of last year's snow. Perhaps there is another meaning to Hemingway's "Snows of Kilimanjaro!"

When we stop to rest among some giant boulders, the view opens up to all sides. Off to one side are the jagged ridges of Mawenzi, Kilimanjaro's other, almost forgotten peak, and down below are the rolling foothills stretching beyond the park gate as far as the eye can see. The Machame Route is indeed as scenic as all the travel guides have claimed. This landscape – wide open vistas but still plenty of vegetation – is my favorite so far. I already regret that we'll soon leave this behind as well.

As I trudge up the mountain taking in the spectacular sights, I fall in step with Dylan and his father, wanting to share my observations. But the two are already having an animated conversation. They are debating the question of who is entitled to wear the black fleece shirt with the cool thumbhole detail.

"It's my shirt."

"No, it's *my* shirt; I was the one who bought it."

"Yes, but then you gave it to me."

"No, after that you said you didn't want it, so I took it back."

"Well, I want it now."

"Well you bloody well can't have it!"

And so it goes for at least 150 meters of altitude. It reminds me of another hike, one that took place almost exactly 20 years ago. Klaus and I, having finished graduate school and taking advantage of a three-month gap before being ensnared by corporate America, had bought an old Ford Aerostar, stripped it of its back seats, thrown in a futon mattress, and pointed it down the next highway to whichever national park struck our fancy. It was a glorious summer. We zigzagged across the American West and one day came to a stop at Bryce Canyon in Utah – the one with all those amazing statue-like stone sculptures or "hoodoos" rising out of the ground. We hiked along its ridges, awestruck by the sights we saw. On one of those hikes we overtook a couple, German-speaking like us and deep in conversation. Completely ignoring the spectacular landscape, they were recapitulating which campground so far had offered the best deal.

"The one for 12 dollars," said he.

"Yes, but that was the one without the shower token," said she. "With the shower token it was more."

"No, I'm quite sure the shower token was included," he retorted.

The exact cost of the shower token seemed to pose an existential and irreconcilable question, and the debate got very heated before we slipped away and out of earshot. I'm quite certain neither one of those two could ever correctly identify a hoodoo if it hit them over the head. They probably don't have any recollection of ever having visited Bryce Canyon.

Perhaps this is a law of nature: the degree of natural beauty around us stands in inverse proportion to the sophistication of our thoughts at that moment. We are all a bit guilty of that here on Kilimanjaro, becoming ever more obsessed with discussing our bodily functions as the terrain has become progressively more stunning every day. At this rate, I shudder to think what might pop into our heads if we ever make it to the summit.

I move on ahead and seek out another group of two. This one, I'm happy to learn, has definitely been inspired to ponder more existential questions. Dudley and Adrian are

engaged in a lively discussion centering on the profound –
and as of yet perhaps unasked – question, *Is an egg suited
well to withstand a vacuum?* I suspect this is not something
that would normally interest the average person all that
much; most people will happily spend their lives without
ever finding out. *What happens to an egg in a microwave*
might be a different matter – a question quite a few
mothers have regretted was ever pondered by their
curious offspring. But vacuums?

I'm immediately captivated. It is the utter uselessness
of such questions that attracts my attention. I love learning
for the sake of learning itself. I'd even say that learning
something new is usually more gratifying than already
knowing it. And you never know, maybe it'll come in
handy after all. I read the other day that mathematicians,
over the centuries, have worked hard at discovering new
large prime numbers, not so much because they thought
they were useful for anything (they weren't, back in the
19th century), but because they were there to be
discovered. And lo and behold, extremely useful was what
they eventually *did* become in the age of the Internet and
the ensuing need for data encryption. Without ginormous
prime numbers (the most recently discovered one has 17
million *digits*) you couldn't purchase a single thing from
Amazon.com, and that would be a problem, wouldn't it?

Who knows, maybe a hundred years from now
they'll solve intergalactic travel with the answer to the egg
problem, which I hate to say we're not exactly solving
today. But we do manage to occupy the better part of the
morning with a lively debate about it until it's time for our
lunch break. We eat our boiled eggs which look very
normal and unaltered and not intergalactic in the least.
(Quick: does it take longer or shorter to boil an egg at
higher altitudes?)

After lunch and a short rest, which we spend splayed
out on the warm rocks, we move on, and the groupings
change yet again. This time I'm among the women, and of

course we immediately gravitate toward our favorite topic, the toilet tent. We agree, especially as women, that hiring Tee-Tee was a splendid idea. There are some feminine needs that are more easily addressed between closed walls. What's funny, however, is that the guys have embraced it just as eagerly. Even Mike seems to have become a quick convert, admitting earlier that he was indeed quite pleased with the privacy provided by our tent. "Boy was I glad to have a private crap" were his exact words, I believe.

Except, perhaps, if one tent is nice, why did no one think of hiring two of them, especially at these bargain prices? It would have been a splurge well worth it, because one of us might have stepped in some human waste – as we've all found out, not a difficult thing to do – and caught a nasty stomach ailment in the process, monopolizing Tee-Tee for two straight days. All of a sudden, Tee-Tee is not such a happy place anymore, even if it happens to be available. You catch yourself wistfully gazing at other groups' Tee-Tees, wondering if anybody might notice if you stole into one of them under cover of night.

Or if you just peed somewhere between the tents.

Because, by golly, you have to pee!

This seems to be one of the side effects of Diamox, which most of us have started taking at various points in time to ward off AMS, or Acute Mountain Sickness. That, and a weird tingling in your fingers and toes and perhaps even other body parts that shall remain unnamed. Despite its side effects, Diamox has proved a blessing to our group, because it temporarily provides a new topic for endless debate. Except that its one major side effect invariably leads us back to our other favorite topic, the toilet.

Diamox makes you pee like there's no tomorrow, to the tune of four times a night or more. This means that at least four times a night, you a) unzip your sleeping bag, b) unzip your inside tent, c) unzip your outside tent, d) fish for your hiking boots or camp shoes, e) crawl out of the tent, preferably without tearing down the tent by tripping over one of the lines, f) gingerly step over boulders in the direction of the toilet, g) zip the toilet tent shut. And then all of the above in reverse after successfully completing what you came to do. (Which, by the way, also involves balancing the roll of toilet paper on your knee while you do your business, should you be so fortunate to have remembered to bring it with you.)

That is a lot of effort just for a pee. Makes you appreciate so much more what you have at home: a clear path to a nighttime toilet visit without any zipping or unzipping actions whatsoever.

The big debate among experts as well as laymen like us is whether to take Diamox or not, and how soon to start taking it. Some people swear by it, and others disdain its use, saying it might even mask the effects of AMS, thereby putting you in more danger. Or, so another argument of Diamox opponents goes, by using it as a prophylaxis you might already have used up one possible cure, in case you do end up getting AMS. Although the only effective "cure" is to get down the mountain as fast as you can (and to acclimatize very slowly before it even gets to that), so I'm not sure this second point holds. Our doctor recommended taking the first tablet even before we started, but we have settled on beginning a bit later, on Day One on the mountain.

Speaking of doctors, you may find that your doctor is not willing to prescribe Diamox, depending on the country you're coming from. This is because Diamox is actually a recommended treatment for glaucoma and some other ailments such as epilepsy, and its use to treat or prevent altitude sickness is not officially licensed everywhere.

If this all sounds terribly complicated, it is because Diamox is discussed extensively in all the Kili literature and everyone seems to have a different opinion about it.

My take is this: While Diamox can't *guarantee* that you will escape the effects of climbing to a high altitude, it does seem to have helped other hikers to acclimatize and to increase their chances of making it to the summit. So why not take it?

The thing is, some people never get altitude sickness and some people do. According to an information sheet by Rick Curtis of Princeton University, Diamox (the name of the active ingredient is Acetazolamide) helps by allowing you to breathe faster, especially at night, so that you metabolize more oxygen. It does this by acidifying your blood, whatever that means. I'm not sure I want to know. The proper dosage of Diamox as recommended by the *Himalayan Rescue Association Medical Clinic*, Curtis goes on to say, is 125 milligrams twice a day, morning and night, starting 24 hours before you go to altitude. I have interpreted this to mean that starting Diamox on the first day of your climb is plenty early, as the first day doesn't take you to any memorable altitude. But maybe I am making this way too complicated. Nowhere does it say that the prolonged ingestion of Diamox might do any harm, unless you count the already mentioned irritating side effects. If you start taking it before embarking on your trip, you might just put your home toilet to a lot more nighttime use.

By the way, I lied just earlier, in that there is indeed another cure for AMS in addition to getting off the mountain – at least a temporary one. It comes by way of a *Gamow Bag*, presumably invented by a fellow named Gamow, which is essentially a portable hyperbaric chamber that can simulate a descent to a lower altitude by as much as 1,500 meters within just ten minutes of being inflated. The patient is placed inside, and his body chemistry reverts to a lower altitude, giving him enough time to then descend of his own accord.

Sounds nifty, right? And indeed some high-altitude expeditions make a point of toting one along or allowing you to rent one for extra dollars. I for one am glad I hadn't ever heard of such a thing, or it might have provided for hours of fretting prior to our trip, like should we choose an operator based on whether they carried a Gamow Bag with them or not, and was I being negligent - if not because of myself then because of Max - if I didn't insist they did? Fretting about the Diamox has been quite enough fretting for me.

Also, the Gamow Bag seems redundant to me. You have at your disposal a perfectly accessible low-tech cure to altitude sickness while on the mountain, which is simply going down immediately when the symptoms are obvious (assuming, of course, that someone can read the symptoms). Why delay it and be zipped up in a bag under what I imagine must be claustrophobic conditions, only to descend a few hours later anyway? If you want to give another porter a job carrying something up the mountain, might as well make it a second toilet tent. You'll get a hell of a lot more use out of that.

Yet another topic that provides for hours of conversation is the eternal debate about feet versus meters. One of us – Mike, who else? – has brought a hand-held GPS that can capture altitude, and, alas, it is set in feet. Every time we take a quick break to catch our breath, he rummages in his bag, retrieves the GPS, and takes the necessary measurements. Then he proudly announces our elevation above sea level – in feet.

"How much is that in meters?" is the inevitable reply, followed by many complicated calculations before the answer is pronounced.

Or Goddy will inform us of the altitude we have achieved today, in meters, and immediately the debate flares up again how much that might be in feet. It's all very confusing, made harder by the fact that above a certain altitude – measured in either meters or feet – your brain seems to slow down dramatically, incapable of performing the most rudimentary math problem in less than ten minutes.

But I don't want to complain too much, because all these exercises of unit conversion are welcome insofar as they distract from our other favorite topic. You know which one I'm talking about.

I'm not even sure why the topic of feet versus meters is such an issue. The only one in our group with a legitimate claim to feet and inches should be Max as the only American-born among us, and he has accepted the superiority of the metric system from a young age. I'm happy to say that eventually Mike will come to see the light and by Day Three the GPS will be switched to meters once and for all.

Because the only number that matters to us is 5,895 meters.

The highest point in Africa.

The height of the highest free-standing mountain in the world.

The Snows of Kilimanjaro.

That's where we're trying to get.

A word about that snow: it's shocking to visualize just how much ice has disappeared from Kilimanjaro since the days of Hans Meyer and those who followed in his footsteps throughout the first part of the 20th century. More than 80 percent of what was there for about 12,000 years until the early 1900s is gone, and the rate at which the glaciers are melting is accelerating. Even Hans Meyer himself, returning almost a decade after his first ascent, was appalled to find that the glaciers had already retreated 100 meters in just ten years. What would he think today?

In 2009 a group of Americans conducted a study for the National Academy of Sciences, and when you look at the aerial photographs they took between 2000 and 2007, you can clearly see – without any background in glaciology – the dramatic decline in ice cover. If it goes on like this – and there is no reason to expect otherwise – the fabled Snows of Kilimanjaro will be completely gone in less than 20 years.

By the way, while on the subject of height, here's an interesting tidbit about Kilimanjaro: its summit is several thousand feet higher than the Everest Base Camp. Doesn't that sound tempting? If you look at it that way, all of a sudden a goal with the words "Mount Everest" in it doesn't seem very far out of reach at all. It would be kind of cool to put *that* mountain on one's "been-there-done-that" list, wouldn't it? Then again, you have to hike for almost two weeks to get to the Everest Base Camp, and it is, as the name suggests, just a starting point for the actual feat, not the destination. Who wants to climb twice as long and almost as high as we are doing it here, only to arrive at a "base camp" instead of standing on a summit? Not to even mention the cold you'd have to withstand in those regions... No thank you – I know why I've traveled to the equator, of all places, to satisfy my nascent ambitions as a mountain climber.

Shira Plateau, when it finally arrives, is a welcome sight. It is indeed a vast plateau, almost level, with plenty of space to allow for some privacy between the different groups arriving one after the other. Once again there is a hut where we are asked to sign our names into the register. There is also the reassuring sight of a helipad marked by a ring of rocks.

And there is a sightseeing program. Not that anyone feels in the mood for another hike, of all things, but we are urged to clamber over some more rocks to the highest corner of the plateau so that we can admire what's known as the Shira Caves. Incredibly, it was only a few years ago that these caves were still regularly used by porters seeking shelter for the night, before the tour operators stopped the practice and made sure that henceforth there were enough tents for everyone, porters included.

It was a long and exhausting day, and we have two guys in our group who are struggling. Martin, whose job has him jet-setting regularly between Australia and America to work on projects on both continents, is suffering from a bad combination of jetlag-induced exhaustion and high altitude. Or maybe that big camera of his has been the last straw. He's been lagging far behind the rest of the group all day, going *mucho pole pole*, and he hasn't said a word since breakfast. Although that's not quite true. In a sign that he's perhaps not entirely at his wits' end, he did utter one single comment. It came at one of our breaks, in response to us repeatedly voicing concern about him.

"I just need to open a can of *harden the fuck up*," is what he said.

The other hiker in our group who is struggling is Dylan. He has spent more time inside the toilet tent than all of us combined. Mike has had to pull several tricks out of his first-aid kit in an effort to stem the tide, and he has even temporarily ceded the hotly contested fleece to his son. I've never seen Mike assume the role of a concerned father, and the fact that for once he *isn't* calling his son a sissy with regard to his lack of strength positively scares me.

Things must be pretty grave.

It's not at all clear that our group will stay together beyond tomorrow.

Shira Camp

Day Three: The First Big Challenge

Shira Plateau to Barranco via Lava Tower, Tue Sept 4, 2012
Distance: 10 km, 7-8 hours
Elevation: 760 m climb from 3,840 m to Lava Tower at 4,600 m, then down again to 3,950 m

Today we make sure to pack all our warm stuff in our daypacks, because it's bound to get cold at Lava Tower, one of the highest points we'll reach this entire week. It's already very chilly in the mornings, and like yesterday we eagerly await the sunrise. No sunshine, no washing or brushing teeth, has become my mantra. It's simply too cold to get any body parts wet. It's a good thing we've had sunny weather so far, or my attentions to personal hygiene might have stopped altogether.

Thankfully, the night's rest appears to have done its job, and everyone is as well rested as can be after a night of at least two trips to the toilet each. It seems as if our group will get to stay together for at least another day. It also seems as if pumping Dylan full of Flagyl (an antibiotic) did the trick. Mike suspected giardia, which is typically caused by parasites in feces. Judging by the not infrequent sightings of, ahem, feces along our hiking trail so far, this diagnosis seems to be accurate. It doesn't matter if it might not hold up in a doctor's office – Mike seems to have picked the right thing from his well-stocked first-aid kit.

I'm beginning to see what a tricky beast altitude sickness is. Many of the symptoms are similar to an intestinal ailment. In Dylan's case, turning around and leaving the mountain would not have solved the problem. It would simply have left the poor boy crouched over a toilet in a hotel instead of a bucket on the mountain, and his dreams dashed to boot. It's a good thing that between the two of them Goddy and Mike have enough experience to have made the correct diagnosis.

Martin also seems to have recovered. I've already seen him walk through the camp and take pictures which he shows to us over breakfast. Aside from a magnificent shot of Mount Meru – its summit glowing pink in the early morning sun while the rest of the world still lingers in semi-darkness – we like the snapshot of Dylan the best: he is standing in front of his tent wearing his boots and twisting his head to get a good view of our toilet porter who – no doubt on Goddy's instructions – is scrubbing the boots vigorously with the toilet brush while dousing them liberally with disinfectant.

We have a long day ahead of us. Even though at the end of today we'll only show a net gain of a little over 100 meters, we'll first have to climb over 700 meters up to the ominous-sounding Lava Tower before we get to descend it almost all again to get to our next destination, Barranco Camp.

The contrast in scenery couldn't be more striking. We set out in what's still more or less a forest (the correct term is moorland, I believe), but within just a few hours the vegetation thins out dramatically and finally disappears altogether. In one long file we wander through the alpine desert, weaving in and out of a sea of large boulders strewn about. For the first time since we started, Kibo seems almost within reach, crystal clear and almost close enough to touch, and the first specks of permanent snow emerge not too far ahead of us.

At some point we cross a lively stream, taking care to step on some rocks so as not to get our feet wet. I'm sure this is the first water we've come across since we left the park gate, and that gets me thinking. Much like everything on this trip, I've taken the magical appearance of water for granted. Our bottles are refilled for us every morning, there's always as much coffee and tea as we want, and we even get that luxury of a bowl of warm water for washing every morning and night. That has to be two hundred liters and upwards a day for the 40-plus people in our group. Makes for a lot of buckets being hauled from however far away the next creek happens to be! I try not to think too much about how brown this creek water looks, and that surely all our water so far must have been scooped out of exactly the same kind of mud puddle. Is that what we've been drinking? I have no idea how the porters get it from brown to clear, just like I have never understood the process of pasteurizing milk. All I need to know is that it somehow seems to work.

As you continue to climb Kili, you begin taking a closer interest in the mountain that all of a sudden is such a big part of your life. There are always those who read ahead on their travels and know every last detail about their destination before they've ever set foot there, but I'm not one of those people. If you already know exactly what awaits you, why even bother going there, is the philosophy of one of my favorite travel writers, Paul Theroux, and I see it the same way. I had only a vague idea where we were flying to and an even vaguer idea of when that would be. It was rather a miracle in itself that we showed up at the airport in time for our flights, because it turned out that we were flying a day earlier than what I had entered in my calendar. There had been a mix-up with the group booking. It's a good thing I have a husband who makes a habit of thoroughly inspecting all e-tickets, even if they're not his own.

I didn't take a close enough look at the tickets nor did I study the exact itinerary of our hike. But now that we are here, we begin to have more and more questions.

Like, "How many people actually make it to the top?"

This turns out to be a very tricky one, and not one your guides will volunteer the answer for. Everyone is here to make it to the top, is their point of view. If you Google this question, the answers are varied. 40 to 60 percent of Kilimanjaro hikers *fail* to reach the summit, it is said. This sounds like a staggering number, but apparently the route you choose makes a huge difference. And here we are fortunate: the success rate for the Machame Route – also called Whiskey Route – is a much more encouraging 80 percent. In large part this is due to the varied terrain and the constant up and down, which has us pulling our hair out most days but is precisely the feature of this route that helps acclimatization the most. Surely the extra day on the mountain - not available on all the routes – is another factor. Lastly, the Machame Route also appears to attract more experienced hikers than the Marangu Route – also called Coca-Cola Route – which has the highest failure rate. It seems that Mike's obsessive planning has been an asset in this respect.

Not that I count myself as an experienced hiker in any way. I'm just happy to piggy-back on the experience factor, statistically speaking.

Oh, and the folks at Coca-Cola must beat their heads in that somehow they got stuck with the route of failure. What a marketing disaster! Then again, perhaps it's worse to have no route named after your product at all. I wonder what the Pepsi people say to all of this.

Since we're talking about drinks: Our route seems to have only one shortcoming so far, and that is the total lack of whiskey, its nickname notwithstanding. Not that I even like whiskey. But don't you think that if a route is called the Whiskey Route there might at least be some kind of alcohol served with dinner? Maybe we should complain to our tour operator after all in light of this serious shortcoming.

Altogether, there are six established routes to the summit of Mount Kilimanjaro: the aforementioned Marangu Route; the Machame Route, which is the one we are on; the Lemosho Route; the Rongai Route; the Shira Route; and the Umbwe Route.

The Marangu Route: Apparently, the Coke reference stems from the fact that Coca-Cola is sometimes available along the route or at least has been in the past. What distinguishes this route from the others, along with the lower success rate, is the fact that it offers actual huts for your accommodation and not just tents as in our camps.

Real huts: such comfort! While that does sound like a nice bonus, it really isn't, when you think about it. It's not like we are laboring every day lugging our tents on our backs and then laboring some more in camp putting them all together. All this is done for us by the porters. And an actual mattress versus my self-inflating mat doesn't get me overly excited either – I shudder to think of all the possible pests such a mattress might contain in its innards.

By the way, there is an interesting side story about the huts along the Marangu Route. It was again the Germans who deserve credit for erecting the first huts, and the name of one of the huts offers a glimpse into the beginnings of the darker chapters of Germany's history. One originally bore the name Bismarck Hut (now Mandara Hut, after the local Chagga chief in the late 19th century), and another was called Peters Hut (now Horombo Hut). The latter reveals a fascinating trail from the days of early colonization all the way to the Third Reich. It is named after Dr. Carl Peters, the founder of the Society for German Colonization who had the reputation of being a bit of a loose cannon during the quest for East African colonization. Barely tolerated by Otto von Bismarck, who had tried to sideline him by engaging in direct diplomacy with the British, Peters nevertheless was elevated to *Reichskommissar* (Imperial High Commissioner) for the Kilimanjaro region in Moshi in the 1890s, where he wasted no time in completely alienating the local population by lashing out with undue brutality. He held himself a mistress from one of the local tribes, and when he discovered her relationship with one of his own servants, he ordered both of them publicly hanged and their villages destroyed. For this misuse of official power he was investigated by the German Reichstag and eventually removed from his commission, but had his title reinstated at the outset of World War I. He was completely (and posthumously) exonerated by none other than Adolf Hitler, who used him for anti-British and anti-Semitic propaganda purposes. It's easy to see why, as Peters was an early proponent of the *Alldeutscher Verband* (Pan-German League), an ultra-nationalistic organization glorifying such concepts as social Darwinism, racial hygiene, and a ban on "breeding with inferior races."

Bedbugs and other hazards aside, I'm all the more glad not to be sleeping in a hut erected in honor of such an unpleasant man.

The Marangu Route is often described as the easiest route, making it also the most popular, because it basically goes upward at a steady clip. The downside, however, is that it doesn't help you with your acclimatization as much as a route that is longer and goes high up and then down again in the space of a day.

Another difference is that on Marangu you use the same route for your descent as the one going up, whereas on all other routes you descend via the shorter – and also steeper – Mweka Route. I'm not sure what to think of that. On the one hand this makes for twice the traffic on the Marangu Route, making it more congested, which is definitely not desirable. What's more, you'll hike down through the same exact scenery you've already seen on your way up. But I don't think that after a week of climbing you're going to be disturbed much by a lack of new scenery as long as you are going down and getting closer to your hot shower and cold beer. Perhaps you'll even see it properly for the first time when hiking off because you were so focused on walking *pole pole* going up that you totally forgot to look around you.

At five to six days the Marangu Route is also the quickest route, making it attractive for those who are on a tight time budget or want to spend less. But frankly, I'd rather take a day longer and spend a little more if that increases my chances of success. It's not like I get to hike Kili every day. Even if you're not bent on reaching the summit, you still don't want to be stricken with AMS, as it can't be very pleasant. While there seem to be quite a few arguments for and against the Marangu Route, the biggest drawback, in my mind, is the route's bad record in terms of acclimatization.

The Machame Route: In the past, the Machame Route was Kili's best kept secret, but in recent years word about its spectacular scenery must have gotten out, because it is now the second most popular route on the mountain. Perhaps even the most popular, depending on who you ask. This seems to play out when we look around us, because lonely we are not. Perhaps people have caught on to the higher success rate as well.

If you look at a map of the mountain, the Machame Route forms a giant inverted "S". The first bend of the S is formed by climbing from the south up to Shira Plateau during the first two days, and then you more or less reverse course for the second bend by hiking halfway around the mountain at almost equal altitude until the final summit push from the east.

As I mentioned, the Machame Route is lauded for its scenery, if not for its whiskey sundowners. I can attest to that. The scenery, so far, has delivered as promised. The views of the Shira Plateau in particular are breathtaking.

Machame is labeled high on the difficulty scale, and therefore takes at least six days. Seven, if you want that extra day of acclimatization, which we do. I have to say I'm not sure what exactly they mean by "difficult." Yes, the ascent so far has been arduous and exhausting, and no doubt two days at the hotel pool with a book on my lap would have been more relaxing, but isn't that the case with all routes? Aside from the fact that we've had to mainly walk uphill into thinner and thinner air, our first two days on the Machame Route haven't been particularly difficult. So far, the most difficult thing I've had to grapple with was keeping my lunch away from the birds and finding a private place to pee without stepping onto anything undesirable.

And swallowing the chlorinated water.

A Coca-Cola sure would make my day.

The Lemosho Route: Rather than from the south like the Machame Route, the Lemosho Route starts on the western side of the mountain and includes a long hike through the rainforest and across Shira Plateau. It's one of the longest approaches. You can make it in six days, but up to eight are recommended.

It's said to be equally as spectacular as the Machame Route, with the same high success rate and grade of difficulty, but much less crowded. All that sounds very tempting, but from today's hike onwards it makes no difference. Once up at the Shira Plateau, the Lemosho Route joins the Machame Route for what's known as the southern circuit through Lava Tower. No wonder it's crowded here – we now have to contend with two routes on one path!

You might also come across an elephant or a buffalo on the first day of hiking Lemosho, adding to the scenic aspect. But also adding, I've heard, the occasional armed ranger to your group, for extra protection.

The drawback of this route is the long drive to get to the starting point. I remember our own bumpy ride from the hotel to the park gate and am not sure I'd want it any longer. Together with the longer hiking time and the need for an armed escort, the remote entry point makes the Lemosho Route one of the most expensive options of scaling the mountain.

The Rongai Route: This is the only route approaching from the northern side of the mountain near the Kenyan border. It's equally as remote and uncrowded (although on Kili "uncrowded" is a relative term) as the Lemosho Route, equally cumbersome to get to, but less strenuous – more of the steady Coca-Cola variety.

It's also apparently the one you want to take during the rainy season, because the northern slopes generally get less precipitation. But wait! Another outfitter warns that during the rainy season the trailhead for the Rongai Route may be impossible to reach due to vehicles getting stuck in the mud. There you have it. One of the more irksome aspects of trying to plan a Kili climb is that you never know who to listen to. There's a ton of contradictory information out there, with each provider trying to outdo the next, and every time you think you've settled on a plan, you'll find out shortly afterwards that this is the worst possible idea ever, if not a dangerous one that will probably get you killed.

As it is, I'm not sure I want to take any of the six routes during the rainy season, so I don't have any misgivings that we haven't chosen the Rongai one.

The Shira Route: Here's a tidbit of information I didn't know before signing up: there is a route where you don't even walk up the mountain, you drive! On Shira, you only catch fleeting glimpses of the rainforest because you are *driven* through it entirely.

As much as my muscles were aching at the end of our interminable slug through the rainforest on Day One, this sounds like a terrible idea. It's as if you're cheating your way up the mountain. Why not hire porters who'll carry you the rest of the way? Or, better yet, go to the summit directly by helicopter?

Then again, if I'm honest, we are all cheating a bit here. None of us started this trek at sea level but at 1,800 meters, which only leaves a bit over 4,000 meters of freestanding mountain to scale.

But there are other problems with the Shira Route. It's harder and more expensive to get to, and it's terrible in the acclimatization department because you go from Moshi to high altitude in just one day, helped by the added transport. For this reason alone you won't find many travel guides recommending the Shira Route. It eventually merges with the Machame and Lemosho Routes anyway, and I'm a bit peeved that we now have to share our path with *two* other routes.

The Umbwe Route: By all accounts this is the most direct, steepest, and most challenging way up the mountain. It has very low traffic, which sounds great, but also a very low success rate, which is less great.

About that traffic: sanitary considerations aside, I think solitude is overrated. I find myself actually enjoying the social aspect of the Kili climb. You meet people, you ask them where they're from, you tell them your story, and you move on. Then you'll likely run into the same people again the next day, or even later the same day, and you share what's happened to everyone.

Or you totally forget you've already met them before and it's embarrassing that they remember your name and you not theirs.

Every once in a while you come across a single guide with just one hiker in his care. The ultimate Kilimanjaro, the private tour, probably purchased at top prices. And yet

I can't help but pity those people. The prospect of a lonely dinner in a one-person mess tent in exchange for our raucous banquets and lewd jokes seems absolutely dismal.

Even if you get the toilet tent all to yourself.

A seventh route, the *Mweka Route*, is one of the most direct routes, similar to Umbwe, but it's only used for the descent after summiting via Machame, Lemosho, Shira, or Umbwe. It's the one we'll be taking down the mountain.

And then there is one other approach, and it's called the *Western Breach*.

I won't get into too much detail about the Western Breach. If you're seriously considering it, you've probably already climbed Kili at least once and might not be reading this book in preparation for your trip. From what I understand, the Western Breach approach has at times been closed due to its higher risks, which stem from more frequent rockfalls than elsewhere on the mountain. It is considered the single most challenging summit approach, and you're only advised to attempt it with an experienced crew. Some of the world's mountaineering big shots have tried themselves on the Western Breach, and it was the legendary Reinhold Messner himself – a household name when I was growing up – who was the first to free-climb the Breach Wall in a direct ascent in 1978.

Somewhere on this rock face you'll reach the point of no return, due to the daily melting of ice keeping the scree together at night and in the early morning, and should anything happen to you past that point, your experienced crew will have to evacuate you up the mountain and over the rim of the crater, rather than straight downhill.

I don't know about you, but phrases like "point of no return" do not exactly arouse my confidence. Who wants "Kili Day 5: Finished hearty breakfast of peanuts and now up Western Breach wall #pointofnoreturn" as their final Tweet? And going anywhere else but downhill in case of an emergency, given the dangers of altitude sickness, seems like a dreadful idea.

But apparently, the Western Breach approach makes up for all this with sheer awesomeness. If planned correctly, it might offer you the opportunity to witness both sunset and sunrise on Uhuru Peak, admittedly a tempting prospect.

I'd like to say that I conducted a complete cost-benefit analysis of all the Kilimanjaro routes and arrived at the Machame Route as the ideal candidate. But, as I've said, I did no such thing. Mike picked Machame, and that was that. And yet I wouldn't have wanted it any differently. As they say, ignorance is bliss: I haven't had to worry my head about any of the 15 ways to die on Kilimanjaro, about getting stuck in the mud on the way, about rockfalls and hypothermia, or about armed guards protecting me from being trampled by a herd of buffalos. Or from being kidnapped for a ransom in rupees, for that matter. All I've had to worry about so far was finding the right size of boulder to disappear behind every once in a while for much-needed bladder relief.

This, by the way, gets harder the higher we go. The vegetation has become sparse, and the rocks are becoming smaller, so that carving out some privacy along the increasingly crowded route is no small feat. The men, of course, don't even bother, but I wonder how many women climbers have had to abandon their bids for the summit due to broken bones caused by overzealous scouting expeditions in this regard. I can't wait to Google it, and figuring out which search term I might use for this is a welcome distraction. (Go on, you know you want to Google it too. You might find an entry for "Toilet-related injuries and deaths" on the ever-reliable Wikipedia, where you might learn that King Wenceslaus III of Bohemia was speared to death "while sitting on the garderobe" in the year 1306, and further inquiry into the origins of the word "garderobe" might inform you that it is very much the same as the *Plumpsklo* of my teenage summers. Not that this is in any way crucial to my Kilimanjaro story other than the fascinating drop toilet connection.)

We pepper Godlisten and Hillary, aka Sir Edmund, with many more questions about Kili routes and geography as we set out on our long trek from Shira Plateau up to Lava Tower. They both know this mountain like the back of their hands and could probably walk all the way to the top with their eyes closed. As I already mentioned, they just came down the mountain a few days ago and turned right around to take us up again the next morning.

While we were at the hotel, there was quite a commotion staged by a somewhat loud American. Or I should say that it was I who dubbed him the "loud American." To all the South Africans present he was just an American. What does that tell you about the reputation of the average American tourist? Anyway, this American was busy promoting (and collecting donations for) his impending attempt to set a new record to scale Kili four times in only 28 days.

By golly, that's a lot!" I remember thinking at the time.

But since then I've had time to see the other side of it. From the guides' and porters' point of view, four times to the summit in four weeks is probably a record that has already been set and broken ages ago based on pure necessity. Some porters even seem to scurry up and down the mountain several times a *day*, they run so fast. So any new record of that nature does not really count all that much, in my humble opinion. As often is the case, the locals are left out of the equation as if they simply didn't exist and as if only the foreign hikers counted.

While we're on records, there is indeed one of them worth noting. Goddy tells us about Lance from South Africa who he says at one time held the record of fastest to reach the summit – achieving it in just 9 hours 45 minutes.

Never mind that it has since been broken (the actual record hovers around a mind-boggling five and a half hours from park gate to summit) – the fact that Goddy personally knows this Lance makes his record seem more real than a mere statistic.

I can't help but be impressed. Here we are, having already walked for almost three days and probably close to 20 hours in total, and that snow-covered peak is as far away as ever. Heck, it'll certainly take us longer than nine hours to walk *down* the mountain again. Lance must have practically jogged up the most direct route there is, and he can't have taken many breaks.

On the plus side, he didn't have to worry about as many potty breaks either.

And I dare say he also didn't have a cellphone to charge, whereas regular folks like us, and especially Adrian, have a burning desire to charge our phones while on the mountain, which for some of us also double as cameras. Doesn't the idea of a mini solar panel to strap to your backpack and connect to your phone so that it can charge while hiking in the sunshine sound like a wonderful invention?

Well, just like communism, it works better in theory than in practice. That little panel Adrian has mounted on his backpack does indeed succeed in producing a charge just powerful enough to wake the phone from sleep and make it chime with a rather loud *da-dinggggg* sound. But that effort proves to be too much for the poor phone so that it immediately falls into an exhausted slumber, only to be woken up again a moment later announcing itself to the world with another *da-dinggggg*. There's a veritable Morse code conversation of insistent bleeps emitting from Adrian's direction. Whenever we rest, we soon follow a pattern: we wearily set down our backpacks, we stretch out on a warm rock to get some much-needed rest and perhaps even doze off for a moment, and then we all jerk up again when the beeping resumes. At some point in time during the week, the solar panel goes the way of the debate about elevation in feet, meaning it is voted off the island (or, in the event, off the mountain). Although, not content to let it go entirely, Adrian is able to re-fit it so it can charge Sir Edmund's camera battery which thankfully has no ambitions to emit any decibels at all. After that, Adrian's quite impressive technical skills are needed in more urgent quarters, namely for masterfully spreading rock-solid peanut butter on David's soft sandwich bread at breakfast.

When we finally reach Lava Tower in the early afternoon, we are utterly spent. It has been less of a climb than either of the previous days, but the thin air is starting to take its toll. The good news is that our only job up here is to rest for an hour and acclimatize to the 4,600 m in altitude as much as we can. The bad news is that this is not as restful as you might imagine.

First of all, the wind is bitterly cold. Finding a sheltered rock to spread out on as flat as possible to soak up the sun's rays requires quite a bit of scrambling.

Secondly, there are the greedy ravens to contend with. As soon as I open my lunch packet I have to focus all my attentions on keeping the ravens at bay. I just have to look away for a split second, and one of those thieving birds is making off with a piece of my sandwich, devouring it on a nearby rock while eying me derisively and planning his next sortie.

And finally, performing our ablutions before settling down to our naps, as ordered, is quite the challenge. I mainly mention this because I have come to love the word *ablutions*. There is no shortage of rocks to squat behind – Lava Tower is basically a huge pile of rocks – but the trick is finding and then climbing to a spot where a) you have privacy and b) over three hundred people haven't already squatted before you and bequeathed the results of their respective ablutions to you without troubling themselves with garden trowels and such.

I wistfully remember the Urinelle and Shewee and all the other contraptions from my research into the female toilet predicament. After three days spent squatting behind rocks I now deeply regret not having invested in one of them.

The guys, of course, have nothing to worry about in this respect. My only consolation is that they have the same travails as the women with their number two business. Because – and this is just a guess – there are no contraptions out there for that.

When we start our descent to go down to Barranco, our next camp, I cannot slow myself down. Max and I practically run down the mountainside. It's such a joy to go downhill for a change, and unlike some other hikers in our group we are not encumbered by any weak knees. We run so fast that we almost fail to notice how rapidly the landscape has changed again. One minute we were up in the bleak but sunlit alpine desert, the biting cold air seeping through our jackets and making us shiver, and the next we are walking through an eerie twilight, surrounded by the most unusual looking trees I've ever seen. They are called senecio trees, Goddy informs us, and this particular genus (*Dendrosenecio*) is only found in the alpine zones of equatorial east Africa, with each species almost exclusively confined to a single band of altitude. Strangely, these trees belong to the daisy family, but you wouldn't guess it. They look like the bizarre outgrowth of crossbreeding a cactus with a palm tree – a bare tree-trunk of a base, looking rather undersized and frail, with thick knobs of branches clustered on top and extending into what looks like palm fronds or aloe leaves. Some of them are truly gigantic and easily hundreds of years old. Immersed in the thick fog we've descended into, these trees take on an otherworldly and slightly disquieting aura. If black

Hunger-Games-inspired flying apes suddenly came screeching at us, I'd only be half surprised.

Just as the landscape has transformed itself so dramatically, so has my mood. What moments ago was a playful race against my son has turned into a gloomy and tiring affair because I can feel a huge headache coming on. With each downward step the pounding in my head increases, as if I am descending into a pressure chamber. The last ten minutes are pure agony. With each new step, my head feels as if it's going to split. I say a silent prayer of thanks when the camp suddenly emerges from the fog, and all I can manage to do is crawl into the first familiar-looking tent, close my eyes, and let Max unpack and go to dinner on his own.

I don't think my head has ever hurt so much in my life. I also feel as if I need to throw up, but the idea of moving even my little finger seems quite insane, so I just lie there trying to will the pain away. It takes me 15 minutes just to form a plan of how to get to the Ibuprofen in my first aid kit. I finally get up the nerve to execute it and swallow some pills, and the effort is so taxing that I collapse again, quite sure that nothing and no one will ever rouse me again.

But I'm wrong. Goddy, who has immediately spotted the empty chair at dinner, unceremoniously zips himself into my tent and proceeds to interrogate me. If he pulled out a stethoscope, I wouldn't be one bit surprised; he has such an air of doctor around him. And quite doctor-like he delivers his orders for me, which encompass dragging myself to the toilet and then to the mess tent, where I'll be expected to drink some tea and eat some soup.

Getting up is the very last thing I want to do, but from the first day every one of us has done exactly what Goddy has told us to do, and so it is this time.

Apparently, getting a headache after Lava Tower is quite the common occurrence. It's part of the acclimatization process, although I would have thought going back down to a lower altitude makes you feel better, not worse, as it did in my case. It's rather odd that only one in our group gets it, and it's rather annoying it has to be me. It'll be much better after an hour, Goddy assures me, and he is right. He almost seems cheered by my exhibition of symptoms he has so accurately predicted, as if he would have been severely disappointed had no one gotten a headache today.

While I do feel better some time later, I still can't bring myself to force down any of the food that has been piled onto my plate by well-meaning hands. The mere thought of peanuts – the last thing I ate at Lava Tower – is enough to make me ill for the rest of the week. I force down as much tea as I can and crawl back into my sleeping bag, teeth chattering.

I know this has been my first big test. I'm a bit worried about Barafu Camp which will take us back to the same altitude as Lava Tower. Let alone what comes after Barafu Camp: the final stretch to the summit. For the last few days, I have tried to push all thoughts of summit night out of my head, because there is nothing we can do about it, and it's not in my nature to fret about things I can't change before they've even occurred. But nevertheless, summit night is our constant companion, simmering just below the surface, no one daring to speak much about it lest we jinx it in some way. Other hikers we meet along the way are full of stories – horror accounts they have read about, friends of theirs who didn't make it on previous trips, people who only persevered with superhuman effort. Up until this point, my only concern in connection with summit night has been that I'd be freezing, that despite layers and layers of clothes and protective gear I'd be shivering to the bone and be miserable.

But what if that'll be the least of my problems? What if I'll feel like this again, not being able to stand up straight, my head splitting with searing pain, all the while having to force myself up a slope so steep everything we've done until that point will seem laughably easy in comparison? I'm not sure that I'll be able to take it.

But first things first. *Pole pole*, one step at a time.

Tomorrow is going to be a new day.

Senecio trees close to Barranco Camp

Day Four: Traffic Jam
in the Death Zone

Barranco to Karanga, Wednesday, Sep 5, 2012
Distance: 5 km, 4-5 hours
Elevation: 250 m net climb from 3,950 m to 4,200 m

Only reluctantly do we open our tents when we hear the wake-up call, as the mornings have gotten very cold. Whatever water you left outside the night before is frozen by morning. Dylan is making everyone laugh by parading his face cloth around, frozen into a solid sheet in the shape it was hung up last night. The peanut butter has gotten so hard it's impossible to spread, which I suppose is why David, who seems to subsist on the stuff, has delegated that task to his father.

I find it oddly comforting to watch Adrian repeat this procedure at every meal, methodically prying uncooperative clumps of peanut butter out of the jar and placing them onto slices of bread laid out in a row, all under the watchful eyes of David, who is reclining in his seat, arms crossed. I'm not the only parent, I'm relieved to learn, who does stuff for their children which they are perfectly well equipped to do for themselves. As much as Max is often embarrassed to merely be seen in my company, he never seems to have a problem asking me to tie his shoes or put on suntan lotion. I know I should've nudged him toward more independence long ago, but at least I'm in good company. Both David and Max would have shown up with only the clothes on their backs if left to their own devices pre-departure. I know this because Andy – David's mother – and I have shared more than one eye-roll over this very fact.

Not so Dylan. Not only was he the one to instigate this whole expedition, he has also been gung-ho about it every step of the way, competing with Mike over who could carry more bricks and pooh-poohing the wussies – meaning the rest of us – who were less than enthusiastic campers. He proudly packed all his own gear, and even if he'd asked Mike for help, he would only have gotten a gruff "You can bloody well pack your own frikkin' gear" in response.

Everybody seems well rested today, including me. I feel like I'm reborn, even though sleep has been hard to come by at this altitude. My headache has completely disappeared, and my spirits have never been better.

It's a gorgeous morning. It starts off cold, but as soon as the first tentative rays of sunshine find their way over the horizon, we can feel the warmth spreading through our bones. The landscape around us looks as if freshly painted, having only revealed itself to us now that last night's fog is gone. We are camped on the floor of a wide valley that is flanked by steep slopes and ridges on all sides. There are senecio trees as far as the eye can see, and the sparkling blue sky high above kindles the wanderlust in the most reluctant traveler. Our spirits are also buffeted by the knowledge that today will only be a short hike, four hours or so, because we are using the extra day on the mountain to break up the trek to Barafu by camping at Karanga. This has been Mike's plan all along.

Even though I'm brimming with energy I can't help thinking back to last night. I don't ever want to have a headache like that again. And yet, according to the experts, what I had only qualifies as a symptom of *mild* AMS, along with a loss of appetite, nausea, shortness of breath, fatigue, sleeplessness, and general malaise, all of which some of us have had at some point or another.

It is said that these symptoms are typically worse at night. This makes me smile. Even though I'm not a medical expert, I daresay that sleeplessness would naturally most often occur at night.

What really should concern you and prompt you to turn around pronto is the onset of *moderate* AMS, one step up from mild. When you have moderate AMS, your headache is severe and won't go away, you're vomiting, you feel very weak, you're increasingly short of breath, even without exerting yourself, and you start to become uncoordinated, a condition called *ataxia*. Do you know what test they recommend to find out if you have ataxia? Walking in a straight line, as if you were doing a sobriety test at a traffic stop. Which I guess is why they're not serving us vodka tonics as aperitifs at dinnertime. You'd never know if it was ataxia or the alcohol talking when you stumble to your tent at night. And, quite frankly, I do enough stumbling over rocks and tent lines during my nightly toilet visits that I don't need any additional impediments.

If you show any of the symptoms of moderate AMS, you're advised to descend to a lower altitude and rest there for 24 hours until you feel well again, at which point you could give it another try. The only problem with that strategy is that by that time your group will be far in front of you. Unless one of the guides stays behind with you and agrees to make another attempt – if he is even qualified as a head guide – you are probably out of luck. Still, descending is your only option. Continuing on after experiencing symptoms of moderate AMS can lead to death – via fluids in either your brain or lungs (the correct terms are HACE for *High Altitude Cerebral Edema* and HAPE for *High Altitude Pulmonary Edema*) – and no responsible Kili guide will let you do it.

Anyone can be stricken by AMS. There is no factor such as fitness or age or gender that makes it more or less likely for you to be affected. Even the same person having no trouble one climb can be forced to turn around the next climb, and vice versa. Being healthy and not battling any respiratory diseases is definitely a bonus. And taking Diamox might help, as I've mentioned already. I've also heard mention of a steroid called *Dexamethasone* that decreases brain swelling and thereby reverses the effects of AMS. It appears that some people recommend taking that alongside Diamox, preventively. But I am rather suspicious of it and haven't brought it along, as it seems to have some possibly serious side effects. I'd rather treat headaches exclusively with Ibuprofen, as recommended by Goddy.

But since we're discussing possible means to counter AMS, what of the obvious, which is oxygen?

Supplementary oxygen definitely helps, seeing as AMS is solely caused by a lack of it. Despite this, it is neither recommended nor widely used. Most guides carry an oxygen bottle for emergencies, but the verdict, should you show severe symptoms of AMS, is still the same: the only thing to do is descend to a lower altitude. Continuing with the help of bottled oxygen only makes your symptoms all that much worse once the oxygen runs out.

The other obvious question asked by many would-be Kili climbers is this: Wouldn't it help to be super fit so as to better withstand AMS?

Apparently not, as I've already glanced from Martina Navratilova's experience. Of course she isn't the youngest anymore, but there are many other examples of professional athletes who've had similar problems on their Kili climbs in spite of their fitness. And then there are people who're rather unfit and have summited without a problem.

I'm not saying that you should – were you interested in a Kilimanjaro climb – spend your months of

preparations gorging yourself on fried chicken and beer
with your feet on the coffee table watching Bachelorette
reruns around the clock. What I'm saying is that you
shouldn't drive yourself crazy trying to get fit. Unless of
course you're planning to run up the mountain at a steady
trot, in order to break the current speed record for a
Kilimanjaro ascent, held by Kilian Jornet Burgada of Spain.
In 2010 he went from base to summit in an incredible 5
hours and 23 minutes, and then ran down again so fast his
total was 7 hours and 14 minutes, setting another record
for the ascent/descent combo.

Speaking of Kilimanjaro records: Almost more
meaningful than the Spaniard Burgada's record is the one
held by Simon Mtuy, a Tanzania native and mountain
guide, environmentalist and AIDS awareness activist. In
2006 it took him 9 hours and 21 minutes to the summit and
back along the Umbwe Route, which is almost two hours
longer than Burgada's time, but he did it completely
unaided, carrying his own food, water, and clothes.

If you're a woman, you might take consolation from
the fact that there's a lot more room for new record-
setting, should you be so inclined. Debbie Bachmann,
herself a Kilimanjaro guide, holds the current female
record of 11 hours and 51 minutes from base to summit,
set in 2011.

What I'd like to know with all these records is how
these guys deal with the problem of acclimatization.
Everyone will tell you that the key to conquering AMS is
to ascend slowly, with plenty of breaks in between. But
when you run up the mountain in five or six hours, there's
no time for many breaks. Maybe it is so fast, I wonder, that
you end up outrunning the symptoms and are down again
before your body realizes what you've done?

I'm sure I'll never find out, because there's no way
I'm able to jog up this mountain even for two minutes.
And all the other records seem to be taken already. I'm
neither blind (like Erik Weihenmayer, who was the first

blind person to climb to the summit of Mount Everest, and who also climbed the other six of the Seven Summits of the world, including Kilimanjaro – his autobiography is a worthy read), nor young enough (that record goes to seven-year-old Keats Boyd of the United States, who must be a lot less whiney than my kids when it comes to walking uphill, and whose parents must have somehow sneaked him past the authorities, considering that the minimum age for climbing Kili is ten), nor old enough (I won't know until a few weeks later, but amazingly, just a few groups behind us are the Kafers, a couple from Vancouver trying to set that record at 84 and 85 years old).

Hold it! I suppose I could still set my eyes on that last one. Will someone please remind me in about 40 years?

This morning, however, we're not thinking about any records. When we step out of the mess tent after breakfast, all we're thinking about is how grateful we are for the warm rays of the morning sun, which has crept up higher into the sky and is bathing the mountain in a golden light. Because the sun feels so good, we mill about for a while and take our time packing up.

Except maybe we should have gotten an earlier start. When we finally get going, we find ourselves at the tail end of a very long line of hikers all waiting their turn to clamber up Barranco Wall, a steep rock face and – from a technical standpoint – probably the most challenging stretch on the mountain.

Here I was hoping to catch a week-long break from the notorious traffic in Johannesburg, and instead we find ourselves stuck for hours in the Kili equivalent of a good old Joburg rush-hour. All that's missing is a gaggle of street vendors hawking trinkets.

Nothing is moving.

Far above us the path is clearly marked by a long line of colorful dots, moving at a snail's pace. We are down at the foot of the wall, wedged between pot-smoking porters and a group of music-blasting Americans. The atmosphere is that of a party, and no one seems to mind the delay. Everyone is chatty and in a good mood, and the jokes are flying. Plus, the guy with the music has a pure 1980s playlist, perfect for a little grooving on the mountain. Only as soon as I start rotating my hips Max shoots me an evil look signaling "embarrassment alert!" and so I stop.

Sharon starts a conversation with one of the Americans. He tells us they're from Los Angeles, and we tell him that we live in Johannesburg.

"OMG, that's such a dangerous place," he says. "When I traveled there a few years ago, two people were actually *murdered!*"

I hear such comments often. It's kind of interesting – South Africans are so used to this, they just shrug their shoulders and move on, I think. It's expats like me who are offended and feel compelled to defend the collective South African honor. I can't let this stand, and so I ask him where exactly those people were killed, because he makes it sound as dramatic as if he was practically entangled in a shooting.

"Just somewhere in Johannesburg," he says.

Does he have any idea how big Joburg is? I can't resist.

"I'm sure that can happen to you in Los Angeles anytime," I tell him. And I'm not just making this up. I recently read that more Americans were killed in Chicago last year than in Afghanistan. Los Angeles can't be that far behind.

I'm not sure whether it was my cheeky mouth or my totally uncool dance moves, but after that the music moves somewhere ahead of us and out of earshot. Goodbye Madonna, goodbye Bruce Springsteen!

While we're standing around with nothing to do, the conversation turns to last night. I missed quite the event, I am informed. I can't believe it! While I was lying in my tent during dinner feeling sorry for myself, who should appear at our very own mess tent for a chat with Goddy? The legendary Lance himself, he of the 9 hours and 45 minutes from gate to summit! He still occasionally leads tours up Kilimanjaro and just happens to be on the mountain now, climbing the same route as we are. So my untimely battle with altitude sickness has deprived me of an opportunity to gather more of Lance's story.

And of getting a good look at Lance in the flesh who apparently is quite the jock, or so Monia tells me.

"Oh la la, zat Lance, you shewd 'ave seen his mussols."

I feel a vague sense of loss – of both music and Lance in the flesh – as I dedicate myself to the task of climbing up the rock face when the line finally starts moving. It's time to pack away the poles and hold on with our fingers. Occasionally, Goddy turns around to lend us a hand. Being the wise man that he is, he only tells us afterwards about *Hugging Rock*, which gets its name from the way you have to carefully shuffle your body around it. Apparently a porter died here last year when he lost his balance and fell into the abyss.

Hiking Kili is not for sissies, I suppose.

At some point in the planning stage I Googled "Death on Kilimanjaro" – just for research purposes, I told myself – and immediately regretted it. I found that around 10 to 15 fatalities occur annually on Kilimanjaro, along with around one thousand non-lethal evacuations. Several of the deaths are caused by AMS, but not even the majority. The porters, it turns out, are the most at risk, mainly due to insufficient equipment or experience. They can freeze to death when caught in a sudden snowstorm, or they might decide to hike a new path on their own without sufficient training.

Recalling the madhouse at the base of the mountain that first day, and the scramble of the porters for coveted jobs, I realize it's entirely possible that for some of them that morning was their very first day of work, and that they were probably wearing little more than flip-flops and a t-shirt. I'm glad we haven't had any sudden snowstorms so far.

Another thought now popping into my mind, unbidden, is the story told by Jacky, who climbed and summited Kili several years ago (though not together with Mike). Like us, her group started out at the Machame Gate, and like us, they had to wait a few hours before the hike began. Unlike us, however, they witnessed a body bag carrying a porter's body being taken off the trail. Apparently he had died from hypothermia. And later, on Shira Plateau, they heard of another two deaths the previous night, both hikers, one of whom had also succumbed to hypothermia whereas the other's fate was unknown.

I'm relieved we haven't heard of any deaths while we've been on the mountain. Then again, with Goddy being our main source of information, I'm sure he wouldn't tell us anyway. He is wise beyond his years.

Some of the tragedies one reads about don't have anything to do with mountain climbing. On May 18, 1955, East African Airways flight 104 departed Dar es Salaam for Nairobi and was never heard from again, crashing into the southern slope of Mawenzi and killing all 20 passengers on board. Had it flown just 10 meters higher, it would have cleared the ridge. In November 2008 a Kenyan Cessna crashed on Kilimanjaro at around 4,300 meters altitude, killing all four passengers. The wreckage can still be seen on the plateau between Mawenzi and the summit.

And some of the tragedies you read about aren't even real. I find it fascinating that there is an entire *Summit Murder Mystery* series of books, covering the Seven Summits of the world and the fictional murders happening on them. *Murder on Kilimanjaro*, which I have on my Kindle, promises to be especially juicy, featuring a tall and slim pickup-basketball-loving, struggling-to-give-up-smoking American president returning to his roots in

Africa. (Some whisper that he was born there instead of the United States, but that is totally not fictionally true.) Honestly, who thinks up such crazy characters? This president wants to fulfill a longtime dream to climb Kilimanjaro, and to meet his until then unknown son from a youthful dalliance with a tribal princess. I'm very intrigued to find out what happens next.

One particular Kilimanjaro disaster stands out from the rest on account of its gruesome details. Remember the Western Breach approach that is so popular among the adventure seekers? On January 4, 2006, a group of American hikers left Arrow Glacier camp to begin their ascent up and through the breach into the crater. At around 5,300 meters, the glacier above them released 30 or 40 tons of rock, caused by the irrevocable melting of the ice. They might have heard it coming in time to scramble out of the way, but it was a windy day with poor visibility and so it must have struck them with full force, at an estimated 113 miles per hour, before they barely had time to look up. Three of the hikers died, and another hiker and four porters were badly injured. The Western Breach Route was closed in the aftermath, and a lot of soul searching ensued. The area was declared a "death zone," but nevertheless has since been reopened with the guideline of keeping your time in said death zone to a minimum by slightly altering the route.

It sounds a little bit like Russian roulette to me. *Hey guys, there are sharks along this beach right here; make sure you don't stay in the water too long, you hear?* It's crazy to continue to climb there when it's such a high-risk area! Especially when there are other perfectly safe routes available. Right?

Well. When you dig a little deeper, you learn that when the team which was tasked with investigating the accident issued their recommendations to the parks board, they identified *other* high-risk areas to "merit close and regular inspection" due to rockfalls. And you learn that among those are Lava Tower and the Barranco Wall. Apparently, we are trapped in another death zone this very instant and any plans of minimizing our time here are foiled by the very real problem that we are still in the same traffic jam we started out with this morning. We can only move as fast as those above us are moving, and we can only hope that they watch where they're stepping, lest they send some loose rocks flying down our way.

If you've been entertaining your own thoughts of climbing Kili, you're probably now cursing me for going on about all these calamities and worrying you to no end. So let me finish it off with this thought: statistically, 10 to 15 fatalities per year seem very low. I have no idea how, exactly, they counted them, but I'm looking around me and seeing a mountain crawling with people from all corners of the globe, young and old, in various stages of fitness. With so many people in one place, the idea of some of them theoretically coming to their end that particular week doesn't seem so outlandish to me. In fact, I'm surprised the fatalities aren't more to the tune of ten a week. I wonder what death rate you'd come up with when researching your typical ski resort or something comparable over the course of a year. I can only surmise that the extreme caution employed by our guides – and, as I hope, by all other guides as well – is keeping the fatalities as low as they are.

The good news is, when you're scrambling up a rock face on all fours, you don't have much time to think any thoughts beyond where to put your next step. Even if "death zone" isn't the first word that comes to your mind when you stand in front of the Barranco Wall, scaling it *does* require a bit of concentration. From all that I've read you don't need any technical climbing skills for the Machame Route, but this particular portion does appear more demanding than anything we've braved so far. It's also a lot more fun, and I can tell that especially the boys are in their element.

Max – who typically hides his true feelings and is not one to talk much – can barely conceal his joy in the face of this new challenge. I haven't seen much of him the last few days, but I know that he isn't particularly thrilled with the slow pace so far. The excitement is missing. You wouldn't really suspect it, but he is quite the thrill seeker. On the one hand, he doesn't like to tackle anything new and untried, especially if it's a social engagement of some sort, and even more so if such an engagement might lead to a longer-term work effort. This might explain why he doesn't have any real hobbies. On the other hand, the few new and untried tasks he *does* set himself are always daring and slightly reckless: He routinely climbs up the highest slides in the waterpark, those that make me dizzy just *looking* at them; he begged forever last year until we let him bungee jump off the Bloukrans Bridge, allegedly the world's highest bridge jump, and a place I still cannot recall without getting sick to my stomach; and after that, he promptly raised the stakes again and asked to go skydiving.

Climbing in particular seems to run in my son's blood. I remember how he was always first up the climbing wall the few times he tackled one as a little kid, and how he'd look down triumphantly without the slightest hint of fear. He seems to have a natural feel for balance and where to put his feet. Many years ago we spent our summer vacation at a hotel where they had a big floating Styrofoam log in the pool, much like one of those contraptions in *Wipeout*. Whenever you climbed on it, if you even made it up, it started rotating like crazy. Max spent hours on that log, arms spread wide and brow furrowed in concentration, always tiptoeing back and forth while all the other guests kept falling off in droves and eventually gave up.

Who knows, maybe the Barranco Wall will be Max's introduction to mountain climbing. Maybe he could make that his hobby.

When we arrive at the top and have taken in the stunning view onto the world below us, we have the crazy urge to first do a bunch of push-ups and then go leaping into the air. I'm not sure where we get the energy. One of us even performs the push-ups with his backpack firmly on. Perhaps pulling it *off* costs too much energy, I wonder? Or perhaps the altitude is getting to us all and we're on the verge of losing our minds.

It's entirely possible.

We definitely seem to have come up with a novelty, judging by Hillary's enthusiasm for taking picture after picture of us as we step to the edge in pairs, holding hands, and jump as high as we can. He'll probably file it away in his "Crazy South Africans" file. We already provoke a lot of smiles and jokes every time we stop and pull out our snack packs.

"Why South Africans always bring so many snacks?" Goddy wanted to know on the first day.

And he has a point. We are fed around the clock. Not only are we fed, we are made to eat. We are constantly watched to make sure that we do, in fact, finish up our plates. There is so much food to go around that I don't think any of us will be losing weight this week, even with all that walking. There is no reason we should feel hungry in between meals, yet every chance we get we descend on our biltong and chocolate and other goodies as if we'd been starved for days.

Some of us have even gone a step farther in the snack department.

"Dad, you gave me the wrong snack!" David called to Adrian a few days ago when we were spread out between some rocks, taking a break.

"No I didn't," Adrian shouted back. "I gave you Day Three."

"But Dad, today is only Day Two," said David.

The rest of us were all sitting there open-mouthed, maybe even salivating a little bit. Between the two of them they had a stash of neatly packed snack bags labeled *Day One, Day Two,* and all the way to *Summit Night,* lovingly prepared by Andy in a perfect harmony of food groups and flavors.

Doing the same for Max and me would not have occurred to Klaus. I can just see him, were I even to suggest such a thing, telling me to pull myself together. But to be fair, it wouldn't (and didn't) occur to me either. Food is just not that important in our family.

Which doesn't mean I'm not a teensy bit jealous, if only for the surprise factor of pulling out different colored treats every day. Maybe I should have packed some snacks beyond the giant bag of dried mangoes, which seemed like such a good idea when I bought it. I admit I'm getting a wee bit tired of dried mangoes. And Max shoots me a murderous look every time I as much as hint at sharing one with him.

Maybe I should have brought better snacks. Then again, I'm not South African. I don't have Voortrekker ancestors who moved into the vast unknown with an armada of covered wagons stuffed full of beef jerky called biltong and teeth-shattering crackers called rusks.

The rest of the way is best described as up and down, up and down, occasionally crossing a creek. While I don't particularly enjoy having to go down, because inevitably that means up on the other end, I do like the succession of panoramic views. The landscape has an alpine character, with a few evergreen bushes, lichen-covered rocks, and small patches of the so ubiquitous *Helichrysum kilimanjari* providing a bit of color against a background of bleak gray-brown ridges, a sea of fluffy white clouds below.

Once again we seem to be extremely lucky with the weather. Apparently this stretch of the climb is often shrouded in dense fog, or worse, whipped by gale-force winds. My guidebook to Kili (the one I didn't read beforehand) mentions this about today's trail: "During the dry season it rains often, during the rainy season it snows often, and hail can come beating down any day."

We have neither snow nor rain nor hail to contend with, and it seems almost laughably easy when we spot tonight's camp after just a few hours, not too far away and straight ahead. What we don't immediately realize is that there is a deep gorge we must first traverse. The climb down is almost as steep as this morning's wall, and just as treacherous. If anything, it might require even more concentration. Once again, Goddy waits until we're safely down by the river on the valley floor before telling us that a man in the previous group fell down on this descent right here, dislocated his shoulder, and had to be taken down the mountain.

Climbing Kili really isn't for sissies.

I am reminded of another one of our family trips last year which also wasn't for sissies: We had signed up for a canopy tour, and I almost fainted when I had to stand on rickety platforms around dizzyingly tall trees and then swing myself from one to the next, much like Tarzan (or rather Jane) of the jungle. As always, Max was the most fearless of all, and he took particular joy in leaning far out from each platform to send me into spasms of agony. If I already panic when leaning over a precipice, I panic even more when watching my kids do it. And of course they know it. But despite my fear of heights I would have given anything to find a similar zipline spanning this valley here, because then we'd already sit in our mess tent this very moment and dip our fingers into the popcorn bowl instead of painstakingly climbing up and down rock faces without an end in sight. There might not be much net elevation in today's climb, but with all the ups and downs, I'm sure we've traversed 600 or 700 meters.

We're glad to get to camp by 2:30 PM and to have the rest of the day off. We might have gotten there even earlier, but an incident involving Mike and Dylan delayed us briefly. The former had forgotten his hat at one of the higher points we rested at, and the latter had secretly stashed it in his backpack, gleefully rubbing his hands and awaiting the inevitable. Sure enough, about ten minutes later and considerably lower down into the valley, we all came to a stop because Mike was in a frenzy.

"Have you seen my hat?"

He approached each one of us, quizzing us whether we'd seen the ill-fated hat. We all knew which hat he was talking about – one of those ridiculous Aussie caps with long flaps along the side – because the day before we'd already had a good laugh about it: Martin, recovered from his jetlag and always ready with his British wit, had sat down across from Mike with his sandwich, taken a long look at the hat, and deadpanned:

"So how did it go for you in the Foreign Legion?"

Everyone but Mike knew that Dylan had the hat, but no one was willing to spoil the fun. We all tried to put innocent looks on our faces.

"What hat?" I asked.

"Can you describe it?" Sharon said helpfully.

"Oh, you mean one of those hats from the Foreign Legion?" Dudley chimed in.

Amazingly, Mike decided the hat was worth going back for. It sounds easy enough, but you've got to understand that on Kili, you don't go back up lightly what you've already come down from. Between all of us, we probably had five spare hats for him to borrow, and yet a special fondness he must have felt for that particular specimen drove him to saunter right back up the mountain. I'm not lying – he did saunter. "Half up the frikkin' mountain," as he described it afterwards. Dylan took his sweet time and waited and waited until Mike was almost out of sight and over the ridge high above us before taking out the hat, waving it in the air, and calling back his poor father.

To his credit, no one loved the joke better than Mike himself. I'm not sure any other father having this trick played on him would have been such a good sport about it. Mike values entertainment and adventure above all else, and while he was climbing up the path again, he was probably imagining in minute detail how he'd later retell the story to his friends over a glass of wine and some biltong. That thought almost certainly made him happy.

The unexpected free afternoon is a welcome treat for us. Everybody goes and does their thing. Some take pictures, some take a stroll – no doubt to check out the competition's toilet endowment – and some take a nap. Not wanting to spoil my sleep for the night, nor being in the mood for even one more step, I plant myself on a big boulder overseeing the sea of clouds below and start writing in my diary. These hours of sunlight are probably the last time I can do this for a while. It's a pity Kili climbs have to be on such a tight schedule. If money wasn't an issue, I would love to linger here for a few days, just taking in the scenery, and having time to think and write.

When dinner is announced, I almost resent the fact that it's time to eat yet again. I somehow want to hold on a little longer to this moment of solitude. That feeling reminds me of my childhood in a way. I didn't grow up in a family where food was a very central theme. My mother was once overheard by her mother-in-law – my grandmother, who was an excellent and passionate cook – to have said that if there was a pill one could take instead of eating, she (my mother) would gladly relinquish all her cooking duties and hand out pills instead; this of course caused great consternation and was the beginning of a family rift of sorts, and the relationship between those equally strong-willed women never quite recovered.

Perhaps as a result of my mother's shortcomings in the kitchen – she was known to rush upstairs from her pediatric practice at the last second when my brother and I came home from school, scratching together a meal within minutes, and in later years most cooking duties were taken over by my father – mealtimes were never very important to me, and I'd often rather stay out and play way past dinnertime. Eating seemed like such a chore.

What I wouldn't give nowadays for someone to do all the prep work and then just call me when it's time to eat. Because, it turns out, eating is not nearly as big a chore as cooking.

While I reminisce in this way, the sun is disappearing fast, the mountain is beginning its nightly freezing regimen, and I discover I'm only too glad to be making my way to the mess tent. Only dinner is standing between me and the warm sleeping bag.

And the bedtime story.

Lately, Goddy has taken to telling us bedtime stories, of sorts. We'll chat to him during the day and suddenly he'll remember a story from a previous hike, and promise to tell it that night at dinner.

So tonight we get to hear the story of Big Mama Angie.

"Getting Big Mama Angie to the summit almost killed me..." he begins. She was in one of his groups several years ago, chaperoning some American college students. As the name implies, she was of rather heavy build. But she was as stubborn as she was overweight, and wasn't to be deterred from getting to the summit.

While everyone had already gone ahead, Goddy had taken it upon himself to stay with Big Mama Angie. She was huffing and puffing up the mountain on summit night and taking a break after every ten steps.

"This was fine for her," Goddy says, "because she was so fat she could never be cold. But I was freezing!"

It was during one of these breaks that he suggested to her that it might be wise to turn around. But she wanted to hear nothing of the sort.

'You've got to understand this,' she told him. 'I've come to this mountain to do one of two things: I'm either going to get to the summit, or I will die on this mountain.'

Goddy, fervently hoping that she wasn't going to die, had no choice but to stick with her, step by agonizing step. The sun rose when they were still far from the summit, and not much later the rest of the group, already having summited, passed them by on their way down. On and on they climbed, more *pole pole* than anyone ever before or after them. At times he had to push her – no easy feat – and to this day he bears a scar from where he fell, knocked over by her girth when trying to pull her along. A fine pair they must have made that day when they were inching toward the summit at a snail's pace, each battling their own demons – Big Mama Angie because of her exhaustion, and Goddy because of the unfamiliar situation of someone else taking the lead.

They did summit that day, sometime after 6:00 PM when the sun had already set again, almost 20 hours after they had started. It must have been a whole new record in its very own category, and one that's probably still standing today. And it was, as Goddy says, the hardest thing he's ever done in his life.

I don't know if this story sounds comforting or scary as we are approaching Summit Night ourselves.

Arrival at Karanga Hut

Day Five: Lala Salama

Karanga to Barafu, Thursday Sep 6, 2012
Distance: 4 km, 3-4 hours
Elevation: 460 m net climb from 4,200 m to 4,660 m

We wake up to the most glorious morning yet. Kibo is right in front of us and almost entirely free of clouds. The soft morning sunlight leaves a rose-colored sheen on its icy dome so that it positively glows. With our orange and gray colored tents lined up right under it, it makes a striking image. For the first time this week it feels as though we're within reach of the summit.

Going from Karanga to Barafu is a relatively easy hike. As I've mentioned before, when you do the Machame Route in six days instead of seven, you go all the way from Barranco to Barafu, making it absolutely imperative to get up very early so as not to be delayed, as we were, at the foot of Barranco Wall, unless you don't mind dragging yourself into Barafu past sunset. But when you have the extra seventh day, you're in no rush. So we take our time with breakfast – there are still more eggs – and leisurely complete the by now perfected packing routine, before we once again start up the mountain, single file, with Goddy in front.

When we woke up there was frost on the ground, and it required some effort to get out of our cozy sleeping bags. Feeling the sunshine now warming our backs is simply wonderful. The incline is not too steep, but nevertheless our guides have slowed us down to a crawl.

They are taking no chances with the altitude. This gives me extra time to look around, and I notice that we have a lot of company. Groups just like ours are snaking up the mountain, one hiker after the other, with little breaks in between where one group ends and the next begins. Even though we are well over 4,000 meters in altitude, there is still some vegetation. Little tufts of grass and even a few lonely stalks of flowers are interspersed among smaller and larger boulders dotting the slope. Little hoodoos, not unlike those of Bryce Canyon, start appearing on top of larger rocks, except that these are man-made – laboriously built stacks of rocks to mark the passing of previous travelers.

It seems as if the going is almost too easy, a three-hour hike to get from 4,200 meters to 4,600 meters – exactly the same altitude we reached when we climbed to Lava Tower. On paper, it looks like a leisurely stroll. Except that when you're hiking Kili, nothing is a leisurely stroll. Even your nightly trip from your tent to Tee-Tee renders you utterly breathless, and the irony is that you have to undertake that very trip ever more often at this elevation. In fact, the altitude and the cold seem to have an inverse relationship to the size of your bladder. Once again, I'm very happy we (or rather toilet guy) brought along our private toilet tent. Upon the suggestion by one of the guys – I think it might have been Martin – we've taken to removing Tee-Tee's top. ("Let's leave the roof off the shithouse tent to try and alleviate the asphyxiating smells" is the phrase stuck in my head; we might resort to crude language on the mountain, but that doesn't keep us from speaking proper and grammatically sound English.) Tee-Tee, now topless, looks ridiculous when tall people are using it and have their head poking out while the rest is hidden from view, if not from imagination. Still, it is infinitely preferable to the alternative – the notorious Kili drop toilets. The ones where you have to squat. After close to a week on the mountain, I can unequivocally say that after you've huffed and puffed your way to the toilet at high altitude, you have absolutely no energy left to squat. What you need is a solid seat to rest on. Although what constitutes "solid" is debatable. The higher we climb on the mountain, the steeper the terrain at our campsites. More often than not, you find yourself perched inside Tee-Tee at an impossible tilt, fervently hoping that the whole thing won't topple over with you on – or rather in – it, which would definitely not be a pretty sight.

Earlier this morning, there was some time left after breakfast, and because sitting still was making me cold, I decided to go check out the toilet situation. Perhaps the solid construction of the camp loos would win me over and help rid my mind of that image of me tumbling down the mountain, tangled up in green, foul-smelling canvas. When I got to the site, I was surprised. There were two toilet shacks, neatly labeled. "Portero Toilet" was painted in large yellow letters on the beam across the door of one, and the other one, a bit to the side, was labeled "Tourist's Toilet." (That's exactly how it was written, bad punctuation and all.)

What do you know, toilet apartheid on the mountain! But one thing I can unequivocally attest to: they both smelled exactly the same. They smelled terrible. They stank. They looked even worse, as I discovered once I'd taken a quick peek inside, careful not to breathe. I backed away, quickly snapped my pictures for posterity, turned around, and walked away as fast as my legs would carry me.

I should mention here that while you're climbing Mount Kilimanjaro, your idea of personal hygiene takes a serious turn to the simplistic. You're very content with the bare minimum. Like brushing your teeth occasionally, washing your face and hands once a day, and rationing the remaining wet wipes for the most pressing needs. I'm happy to report that it is indeed possible to wash yourself with one wet wipe while in your sleeping bag.

And here's the thing: I quite enjoy this part of our adventure, contrary to all expectations. This morning, I realized with a start that I hadn't looked into a mirror in five days. I've always been very obedient at following instructions, and since the item *(1) Hand-held mirror* didn't appear on my packing list, I didn't bring one. And I haven't missed it one bit. If anything, going mirror-less makes you feel better about yourself. Do you know how often we stare into a mirror on any regular day? And how often we find fault with something or other we glimpse there? I'm not big into hair care and make-up anyway. There's only so much time in each day, and I usually find better things to do with it. Overseas visitors at our house are always baffled when I can't supply them with a hairdryer. I don't own one. My daughters are probably scarred for life, because I don't know what to do with their hair beyond a simple ponytail. The other day, one of the girls had to go to school as a character from *Little Women* as part of their Read-a-thon, and she begged me to put her hair into two braids, and to roll them up into those old-fashioned buns above the ears. How is this physically possible, I ask? Let's just say the exercise resulted in a lot of lost hair and a flung hairbrush.

But I digress. All I want to say is that even if you take a "beauty lite" approach to your appearance – as I do – you are still obsessed with mirrors. And you don't realize that avoiding looking into them might make you a happier person. It's hard to explain, but you gain a new sense of self-worth if you're so unencumbered by the criticism of the one person always harshest on you every single day of your life: your own self. You start seeing yourself in a different light when you stop seeing yourself in the glare of the looking-glass, so to speak. Perhaps this is so because you simply stop thinking about your own person so much when you aren't reminded of it so often.

I should mention though that the one personal care routine I can't do without is brushing my hair. I've become quite obsessed with brushing my hair both morning and night, before hiding it again under the beanie. (I've also become quite obsessed – if not fallen in love – with my beanie; it won't be much longer before I'll start talking to it, much like Tom Hanks talks to "Wilson" the volleyball in *Castaway*. Even though our mountain feels more like an ant hill than a desert island, we've grown inseparable, my beanie and I!) If I can't wash my hair, it has to be brushed. Leaving me regularly with big wads of hair in my brush that I then have to dispose of by burying them deeply in our communal trash, lest they go flying off into some other hiker's face. I'm not sure how other women deal with the hair issue, but all I can say is that if you're female and planning a Kili trip, make sure you bring a nice hairbrush.

The mountain is quite busy this time of year. I knew that already. But I realize I had no idea what that meant until now. At this point, three or even four of the six routes have merged into one, and it shows. There are people everywhere, and sadly they are leaving their mark. The amount of carelessly discarded candy wrappers, hand warmer pouches, and even plastic bottles, is simply disgusting. And yet time and again we also come across those neatly stacked man-made stone towers, crooked and still beautiful. You could get lost pondering their symbolism and all that unites us as people. Art and trash, right next to each other. Perhaps this mountain is like a miniature of our world with all its wonders and flaws, and the higher we climb, and the smaller the space around us grows, the closer everything – good, bad, and sometimes just inexplicable – gets squished together.

I have never understood what compels people to do that. *You bring it in, you take it back out*, is what my mother drummed into me and my brothers from a very early age. It's safe to say that in all my life I haven't left more than a sliver of man-made material out in nature. (Okay, I guess you can call me a hypocrite when it comes to man-made you-know-what, as I'm happily letting someone else handle that.) But why do people have to throw their trash onto the path? When their fancy outdoor apparel boasts at least 25 zippered pockets, you'd think they could spare one or two of them to temporarily host a few candy wrappers, until such time as they reach camp and can transfer it to the communal trash bags, which the porters collect and carry down the mountain.

As anyone can imagine, solid waste is definitely a problem on Kilimanjaro. It's not even as bad as it could be, because a person can only carry a limited amount of stuff on their back so that pure self-interest limits any unnecessary packaging to a minimum. From what I've read, Kilimanjaro is doing better in the litter department than other popular hiking sites. And you could argue that a few candy wrappers won't make a big difference. Even so, what does get left behind on the slopes of Kilimanjaro is a staggering amount, somewhere well over a hundred tons a year. I've read that it has gotten better over time, at least on a percentage basis. Trekking-it-out schemes have been instituted by the Tanzanian park management, whereby guiding companies get some type of reward for carrying waste off the mountain and delivering it to collecting stations. I've also read that there are rubbish weighing stations at all the huts and some campsites (I haven't noticed any so far but also wasn't looking for them), where guides must have their rubbish weighed on a daily basis to make sure none of it gets dumped prematurely. Indeed that sounds like a good program, but more can probably be done – we just each have to play our small part.

The irony of course is this: The very "Snows of Kilimanjaro" we are all coming to see are threatened by climate change – the climate change our habit of throwing away stuff so we can buy shiny new stuff is at least partially responsible for. You would think that most Kili climbers are at least mildly environmentally conscious, but those candy wrappers don't give me much hope.

I admit I haven't much pondered the problem of trash on mountains before this trip, but it makes for some fascinating reading. There's an annual pilgrimage of sorts called *Eco Everest Expedition*, a group of seasoned climbers that have gone up Mount Everest every year since 2008 to remove trash from the base camp and the path to the top. Most of it is made up of discarded oxygen bottles, tents, and tin cans from decades past, or whatever else is left behind in an effort to save much-needed strength. So far, they've collected "over 13 tons of garbage, including several kilos of excrement and a few corpses," according to the Website *Worldcrunch*.

Excuse me, corpses? I had to re-read that sentence three times to make sure I hadn't made it up. That particular type of human waste, in a sense, has never entered my consciousness before, and I wish it hadn't now. It's not an image you can easily get out of your mind again. At least it immediately replaced the image of "several kilos of excrement" before that could fully take hold. I suppose it's a consolation that at that altitude everything is frozen solid, but it doesn't make it any less macabre.

Maybe candy wrappers aren't so bad after all.

As we approach the last (and highest) camp of our ascent, the landscape becomes barren. We've left the last specks of grass and thistles behind and are now walking along a ridge flanked by a large field of what looks like ash. The colors around us have been reduced to muted tones of brown and gray, matched by the ominous clouds that have started rolling in.

We've crossed paths with Lance's group more than once, and each time Monia chirps "Laaaaaaance" delightedly. They are snaking up just as slowly as we are, which leaves me slightly disappointed. I would have loved to see the amazing Lance in action scaling Kili at a clip of 9 hours 45 minutes again, muscles rippling under his tight shirt. Or, better yet, entirely shirtless. That would be a sight to behold.

I'm not quite sure why I take such guilty (and yes, I do feel slightly guilty) pleasure in imagining other men without their shirts on, particularly men I haven't even met. But Monia – who like me has left her husband behind – seems equally preoccupied. Perhaps Kilimanjaro has some kind of libidinous effect on whoever enters its realm? I do know that the local Chagga people have legends about the spirits dwelling on Kilimanjaro, some of them kind, and some of them bent on destroying anyone climbing beyond a certain limit. But none of those tales, as far as I know, mention any spirits of a prurient nature. Maybe it's just a matter of having so much time on our hands for idle thoughts – a luxury most of us don't have in our normal lives. If you have a lot of time to think, I suppose, you're bound to arrive at *that* topic sooner or later. Or perhaps this is yet another side effect of Diamox!? It wouldn't surprise me one bit, given all the weird reactions we've already catalogued. But in that case, judging by the quantities of the stuff we've all swallowed, our group must be one horny bunch.

The view, when we arrive at Barafu around lunchtime, is breathtaking. If, indeed, you have much breath left to be taken from you at this altitude. We're back at 4,600 meters, about the same as we briefly achieved on our third day at Lava Tower. From what I've gleaned when listening to previous debates between Dudley and Adrian, our science gurus, the oxygen content has now dropped from 21 percent at sea level to less than 12 percent. Although I'm not quite sure if that means there is still the same amount of oxygen in the air, and due to the lower air pressure you just end up with less in your lungs each time you breathe, or if there are indeed fewer oxygen atoms in relation to whatever else makes up our air. But it hardly matters. You'll definitely know something is amiss, even if you can't quite pinpoint it. By the time we reach the summit, the oxygen content will have shrunk even further to 10 percent. That's a whole lot less air than what your body is typically used to.

We do get a good long look at the surrounding scenery, plopping down right where we are. For the first time this week we have to wait for our mess tent, not because our porters have been slacking off – they've been here hours before us, as always – but because the spot they have their eyes on is still occupied. Barafu is not the ideal campsite by any means. If you had the luxury to pick from a range of suitable places, this one wouldn't make the cut. It is very steep and sits amid a wasteland of rocks and scree, and it's a miracle there's even enough level ground at all to pitch our tents. Or perhaps not a miracle, but the result of hours of hard work previous porters have put in to dig level platforms into the mountain. Because of this, there is only limited space for a group like ours, and we have to settle down to wait until the previous group's tent is taken down. These guys have summited last night and come back this morning, or perhaps just now, judging from the look of utter exhaustion on their faces. One of the women looks to be in no shape to move on, but we refrain from talking to them. We don't need any horror stories so shortly before our own ascent, and in any case there is nothing we can do to help.

The other group eventually departs, and once our own tents have been put up, we busy ourselves with the usual afternoon camp activities. We let the self-inflatable mats self-inflate, we roll out the sleeping bags on them, we deposit the empty water bottles outside of our tent so that the porters can fill them for us later, and we put everything in its place for the night. It pays to be organized, at least when it comes to three things: your headlamp, your roll of toilet paper, and your camp shoes or boots. There's nothing worse than rearranging the entire tent in the middle of the night because you can't remember where you put your headlamp. We've also learned that it's best to put everything inside the tent, or the ravens make a mess of whatever you leave outside.

If there is one item I sort of regret not having brought along, it is a pair of Crocs. Mike uses them for his camp shoes, and every time I see him milling about, I let my eyes linger with a twinge of longing. On the Crocs that is – just to be clear. I have a perfectly fine pair sitting at home in my closet, pink and fur-lined, and it's especially this second feature that makes me miss them that much more. My nightly trips to Tee-Tee would be so much more enjoyable if they were made on feet wrapped in such luxury. And being Crocs, which practically weigh nothing, they would not have added anything substantial to my duffel bag allowance. It's not that my boots are terrible to wear in camp. They are comfortable and everything. It's just that I didn't exactly foresee that I would have to meticulously tie them every time and tuck away the laces, all in the dark, just to make absolutely sure a stray trailing lace does not – how shall I put it? – pick up any unwanted matter.

Every morning the same routine is repeated, in the reverse order. Rolling up the self-inflating mat, and stuffing the sleeping bag back into where it belongs, is a bit more cumbersome than simply letting everything billow out of its confinement. What's more, I get to do all this twice in a row, as somehow Max has managed to pretend – it's a trait the men in our family have mastered to perfection – that he absolutely, positively cannot accomplish such a difficult task. At least he's not sitting there playing Angry Birds on his iPhone while I labor away. He is also not spending long stretches in the privacy of the toilet, considering there is no privacy to be had there whatsoever ("Anybody in there?" is usually the call that interrupts any reverie you might have inadvertently fallen into), nor is he taking interminable showers. We are spending more time with each other than we have since he still clung to my legs as a three-year-old, although it's not like we're having long meaningful conversations. Our talks are more to the tune of "Time to get up!" and "Do you have any more wet wipes?" and "You should've packed more Bar-Ones!" Still, I wouldn't miss this for the world. Simply spending time like this together with your 16-year-old son is a rare treat.

Having finished our evening routine early, we sit with our backs against the slope in the late afternoon sun, taking in the view. It is the most spectacular yet, and we've already enjoyed great views. Far in the distance toward the southwest we can see Mount Meru (4,565 meters) poking through the thick bank of clouds below. For the first time this week, it seems as if we're actually looking down on it, as indeed we are from our vantage point at 4,600 meters. The summit of Kilimanjaro is right behind us, to the north, obscured by the steep slope rising straight into the sky right at the edge of camp. We can see rugged Mawenzi on our left side, to the east, looking dark and foreboding. Its name means "broken top," a fitting description. Its serrated ridges almost look like a scene from an animated movie, like the mountain hideaway of some evil witch and her cohort of flying apes.

Indeed, we can now make out an enormous creature emerging from the shadows of Mawenzi, circling on the updraft in wide turns. Rather than an ape, however, it is a large eagle, dark-winged, copper-breasted, and with a few feathers hanging down behind its beak. It must be a bearded eagle, also called bearded vulture, we are told. Their preferred habitat is precisely the terrain we have here: craggy ridges and precipices at high altitudes. They have been spotted as high up as 7,300 meters on the slopes of Mount Everest. In Persian mythology, bearded vultures are considered a symbol of luck. Will this one bring us any luck tonight? It doesn't matter – we already feel extremely privileged to have an opportunity to see one as clearly and close-up as this.

It is utterly peaceful up here. You are so far removed from everything back in your normal life, both literally and figuratively. You are floating above all of it, the world at your feet, and all of its problems hidden under a layer of clouds. If I'm not to reach the summit, having reached this place should be enough.

I'm startled to have this epiphany. I'm quite sure that I genuinely feel this way, and that I'm not just repeating a well-worn cliché to myself. These last five days have enriched my life in a way I never thought was possible. The companionship. The sense of being there for each other, trusting each other. Having simple things to worry about, rather than big things, just like I envisioned before our climb. The daily dose of carefree laughter. And yes, the fresh air. All of these aspects of our journey will stay with me long beyond this week, regardless of the destination – of that I am certain.

We watch the vulture a while longer as it soars above us while Martin captures a few good shots of it with his camera, but when the sun starts disappearing behind the western ridge, turning the temperature instantly to freezing, we stumble toward the mess tent and its relative warmth. We really do stumble. The terrain up here is tilted at an impossible angle, and wherever we go we have to climb over unwieldy rocks, slipping and sliding on the loose soil. It's not an easy feat when you are constantly out of breath.

One puzzle has nagged at me for a while: the question about the naming of all these peaks, and the origin of the word Kilimanjaro. That snow-covered peak we've been looking at ever since we got above the clouds at the end of Day One, and the one originally conquered by Hans

Meyer, is actually called Kibo, meaning "snow" in the Chagga language. Then there is the aforementioned Mawenzi, which no one ever seems to climb up, perhaps because it's slightly lower, but also because it's extremely difficult to scale. It was ignored for the longest time while everyone was so busy scrambling up Kibo. It was nearly a quarter century after Meyer's feat before anyone managed to stand atop Mawenzi, which was accomplished by another pair of Germans, Eduard Oehler and Fritz Klute, in 1912. Ironically, they gave this peak, the one Hans Meyer *didn't* scale, the name "Hans Meyer's Peak."

It is almost exactly one hundred years later that we are climbing Mount Kilimanjaro, but we are actually trying to reach the summit of Kibo. If we ever do get up there, we will be standing on Uhuru Peak. Uhuru Peak once actually bore the lofty name of "Kaiser-Wilhelm-Spitze," bestowed by Hans Meyer upon conquering the summit in a tribute to the German emperor. Incredibly, the term apparently stuck until Tanzanian independence in 1964, when it was finally renamed (Uhuru means freedom in Swahili).

Why this mountain has to have so many names, I don't know. To give us yet another topic to talk about? As for Kilimanjaro, Google and Wikipedia don't give conclusive answers at all, so I'll go with what Goddy tells us. We have trusted him with no less than our lives this week, so surely we can trust him with all other matters. Goddy says that in Swahili it means "Shining Hills" derived from *kilima* for "hills" and *njaro* for "shining" or "white."

That settles that. It's a lovely name, *Shining Hills*, just as this mountain deserves. Even if it might not be etymologically correct.

While we're on the topic of language, if the ten of us all came to Kili with one big goal in our minds, Goddy is pursuing a second one with equal tenacity: teaching us as much Swahili as he can. Never mind that the phrases he teaches us don't seem to make much sense whatsoever. He doggedly repeats them for us day in, day out, and quizzes us on them at night before bedtime. Like *Poa kitchisi komandisi nana frigi* – something about a cool breeze and a banana in the fridge. I admit my Swahili spelling skills are probably not up to par, but see what I mean? Because there's nothing much else to distract us, and because we're always happy to be distracted from our toilet obsession, we humor him and learn to say things like *asante sana* (thank you), *karibu sana kaka yangu* (you are welcome my brother), *lala salama* (goodnight), and something that sounds like *cashew asebui* that none of us can ever remember. And of course, since we're in Tanzania, lots and lots of *hakuna matata's*.

I find that I love Swahili. It's a beautiful language, pleasing to the ear, and it sounds especially charming when Goddy, and sometimes the other guides, are singing to us. We get treated to a goodnight song almost every evening, a routine we have all come to cherish without exception, a sentimental and fitting transition to our hard-earned rest. Whenever the time has come to sing, Goddy, Hillary, and the other assistant guides Naiman, Monday, and Peter line up at one end of the mess tent and start their a cappella performance.

Tonight's song is a sort of pre-summit prep routine. I'm guessing it has a biblical theme, as most of Goddy's singing seems to be religiously inspired, but he also liberally adds verses as they pop into his head. There's definitely a verse in there making fun of our South African snacking habit. The five of them sing and dance and make gestures stuffing their faces full of food and almost topple over laughing at their own joke. When they are finished, they bid us goodnight with many *lala salamas* and disappear into the other "room."

I would guess that in a world far from any summits, Goddy would make a fine psychologist. Or therapist, mentor, life coach... He always knows exactly what we need to hear, and what is better left unsaid. Instead of giving us a lengthy lecture about the upcoming summit attempt, scaring us shitless, he opts for an evening entertainment program to help us relax.

Practicing your Swahili also comes in handy when you're lying in your tent at night, unable to sleep. Which I can assure you happens a lot. Sleeplessness is your constant companion on Mount Kilimanjaro, along with the peanuts and the toilet talk.

You're sleepless no matter what kind of sleeping bag you brought, but it's still nice to have a good one. It's one thing to lie awake with nothing to do, but if you have to do it, you want to do it being toasty warm, rather than mummified in every piece of clothing you own, with your teeth chattering. I'm glad to have invested in a pair of good down sleeping bags by First Ascent for Max and myself. They have a minus-eight degrees Celsius temperature rating, which we've further improved on by inserting liners, and we haven't been cold in them so far.

Monia, on the other hand, has told me that she has been freezing in her sleeping bag ever since the second night. She is using an older model (made from duck down instead of goose down) and she sorely regrets not having bought a new one. Every night she puts on all her warm clothes before crawling into her sleeping bag, and still she can't get warm. Apparently her sleeping bag also lacks a hood, and particularly the hood is essential for keeping the warm air inside.

By the way, you can't just rely on the temperature rating and assume you'll be warm. It just denotes the lowest temperature you can still survive at in that particular sleeping bag. Seeing as I am an expert at feeling cold, you should listen when I say that merely *surviving* is a far way away from being comfortable.

It also helps (in addition to saving us money) that Max and I are sharing our tent. The more people mill around in a tent, the more body heat accumulates in it.

Perhaps Monia shouldn't have made such a fuss that first evening about moving in a tent with Martin! If Klaus had come with us, I would have zipped our two sleeping bags together, because it's the warmest way you can sleep. Max, of course, would never agree to this – which is why I wisely refrained from even suggesting it – but with an eye on joint family vacations in the future I made sure I bought the matching sleeping bags: a "right" one and a "left" one, each zipper lining up with its counterpart. It would be a minor disaster, wouldn't it, to find yourself on a frigid camping trip in your cozy tent, ready to hop in the sack with your spouse, as it were, and be tripped up by zippers that don't line up.

Following this line of thought, it occurs to me that sharing a sleeping bag provides a whole new set of entertainment opportunities whenever suffering from sleeplessness, ones that might be more enjoyable than practicing your Swahili. Now that I've alighted on this wonderful new topic, I will let my wildest fantasies – I'm not saying they're about Lance, the mountain climber, but it *is* a possibility – run wild as I stare at the canvas above me.

Lala salama!

Day Six: Lonely on the Roof of Africa

Barafu to Uhuru Peak, very early Friday Sep 7, 2012
Distance: 5-6 km, 7.5 hours
Elevation: 1,235 m climb from 4,660 m to 5,895 m

I can't sleep and cast an occasional glance at my watch, but time seems to be standing still. I fervently wish summit night would start already, but it won't until shortly before midnight (technically, Day Six begins on the late evening of Day Five) and we still have a few hours to go. We were told to go to bed early so that we would get some rest during this short night, but just like the last few nights I woke up again after a short nap and have since been turning from one side to the other. I've sort of gotten used to the hard ground, but tonight the terrain also has an uncomfortable pitch. When we settled into our tents this afternoon, it seemed to make the most sense to orient the sleeping bags in such a way that our heads would be facing up, but now I find myself constantly crawling uphill so that my feet aren't squeezed against the cold seam of our tent.

Max doesn't seem to be bothered by any of this. He is lying next to me, sleeping like a baby, the hood of his sleeping bag cinched tight around his face so that I can only see his nose. Although he wasn't feeling well this afternoon, like a typical teenager he seems to be able to sleep anytime and anywhere without a problem. I envy him, because the wait is torture. My heart is beating like crazy as I stare into the darkness and try to imagine what lies ahead. Goddy tells of people who have fainted up here, not because of altitude, but because of the sheer terror the prospect of summit night stirred in them.

Just as during the previous nights I spend agonizing moments weighing two equally unattractive scenarios in my mind: I'll either have to heroically suffer the increasing pressure on my bladder, or I'll have to bite the bullet and unzip my sleeping bag, find my boots and jacket and toilet paper, unzip the tent, crawl outside into the freezing cold, and navigate my way over big boulders and all the way to where the toilet tent has been pitched. So far it has always been my bladder that gave in first, but up here the idea of a nightly excursion is particularly uninviting. At this altitude and in this thin air, getting to Tee-Tee will cost me all my strength, and once I've safely let myself inside and sat down on the bucket, I'll be teetering at an alarming angle like the leaning tower of Pisa, trying not to capsize. And I'll also have to suffer what Jacky, recalling her Kili climb years ago, has aptly termed "a cruel exposure of flesh to the elements."

I distract myself by thinking back to the days leading up to now. How we started at Machame Gate five days ago, a time and place now seeming to belong in a different chapter of my life. How we snaked up the mountain day after day, *pole pole* and full of confidence and good spirits. How we've met other people on the mountain and heard their stories of what led them here. How summit night always seemed something abstract and remote, something to be dealt with at some later time.

But now it's almost here, the long-awaited summit night, and I'm glad. In the same way that I was glad, as a child, when the hour of the dreaded dentist appointment had finally arrived so that I could get it over with and stop being afraid. I'm glad, but I'm almost shaking with apprehension. What makes it so bad is that you have no way to gauge what summit night might truly feel like. People who've done it will tell you it's hard. But *how* hard?

The butterflies in my stomach wouldn't be so bad if I wasn't also feeling weak. Due to the altitude I haven't felt like eating anything all day, although our guides have done nothing all day but order us to eat, again and again and again. It was hard enough to make sure we drank the required amount of water. I imagine it's probably even worse another 1,300 meters up the mountain. Because that's how much there is still left to go.

Finally, after a near eternity, I hear footsteps and Goddy's voice outside, and I spring into action, relieved that the wait is over. I wake up Max, even though I'd like nothing more than to let him have his sleep, here in this warm and sheltered place, and in silence we begin our preparations for the last time. We put on layers and layers of clothing (in my case, that means my long underwear both top and bottom, a medium-weight fleece shirt, sweat pants, a thick fleece jacket, outer shell pants and jacket, two layers of socks inside my boots, Gore-Tex ski mittens, my beanie, a balaclava, and my jacket hood cinched tight around my face). We strip the backpacks of all but the most necessary items. We have trouble focusing on which might be the most necessary items. We make sure the hoses from the water bladders are tucked inside the backpacks because otherwise they will freeze. We pack my camera and a backup camera. We stuff as many packets of "hotties" in our pants and jacket pocket as we can fit, and then we open the tent flap and step out into the freezing night.

It's already quite busy between our tents. Everyone checks their backpack one last time, tucks water bottles inside it, and puts their hiking poles within easy reach. Especially tonight they will be absolutely essential. I walk around and dispense hand warmers, as I've brought enough to supply an army. I urge them on everyone, except Mike, who flat-out refuses to use anything "that's for wussies."

"Besides," he tells me, "my idea of a *hottie* is something different." I laugh out loud. This is so typical Mike. He glances at me sideways, as if evaluating my "hottie" potential. But apparently, after five days of bath-by-wet-wipe and near-constant beanie-wearing and being bundled into every single piece of clothing I've brought so that my form is approaching spherical dimensions, my hottie appeal is found lacking.

"You can't stuff that kind of a hottie in your pocket," he sighs wistfully and continues to lace his boots.

Before setting off we are served a small breakfast (if you can call it a breakfast at that time of night) of cookies and tea, which we try to force down against our will. Max refuses to eat, suffering from stomach cramps. I file this information away and give him an Imodium, glad to have packed some, but I do not connect the dots. He's also complaining that I'm making him wear too much and that he's hot. We've had this debate for, oh, the last five years, and I've learned long ago not to argue. Nothing out of the ordinary there, is what I'm thinking.

At 11:30 PM, on the dot, the time has finally – finally! – come. On Goddy's command we assemble outside, don our backpacks, and start walking, eyes and headlamps firmly trained on the feet of the person in front of us. That's all that will matter for the next seven hours: the two feet in front of you. Whatever they do, your feet will have to do. It's as simple as that. But of course nothing is ever as simple as it looks and I can't help feeling weary.

Slowly we begin the long trek up to the summit, the ten of us, plus five guides. Goddy, as always, is leading the pack, at an even slower pace than usual, if that's possible. *Pole pole*, and then *more pole*. We're walking so slowly we're almost standing still. And even so, we have to stop often to catch our breath. Just standing still is exhausting.

After only five minutes of walking, my toes are frozen solid. I can no longer feel them and am struggling to keep my fingers from the same fate by constantly wiggling them, which isn't easy while trying to hold on to my hiking poles. So much for those hand and toe warmers. They do emit heat, but it's no match for a cold, clear night at almost 5,000 meters. Or maybe they're just too old and have lost their power.

You know how they say that hiking downhill is harder than hiking uphill? Well, they're lying. Or they haven't attempted to summit Kilimanjaro yet. This is hard. Sooooo hard. While I carefully set one foot in front of the other, I train my mind on two thoughts to keep me busy. The first is this:

What the hell was I thinking?

What is wrong with the *southernmost* point of Africa, which I've already seen and which was perfectly easy to reach? Why in God's name did I have to focus on the *highest* point? Thankfully, this line of thought provides a few moments of distraction, because I now remember that, technically, the Cape of Good Hope is not even the southernmost point of Africa. That distinction goes to Cape Agulhas a few hundred kilometers more to the east – a fact that Max had pointed out as we all proudly stood at the Cape of Good Hope signpost, hair blowing in the fierce wind, when as usual he had been the only one in our family who'd taken the trouble to research the topic properly. So I can only claim the dubious feat of having stood on the south-*westernmost* point of the African continent. But let's not split hairs here. At this stage, I'd gladly walk all the way to Cape Agulhas and back instead of up this slope.

My second thought is this: *Why do we have to do this at night in what must be minus-20 degrees Celsius, when it would be so much more pleasant in the sunshine?*

I suspect I know the answer already. No one in their right mind would keep going in the daytime, when you could see the steep mountain ahead of you, how far it stretches, and how insurmountable it is. You'd take one good look, shake your head with incredulity, say "no thanks," and turn around, pronto. Perhaps the guides, in an attempt to forestall such mutiny, use the cover of night to veil the true dimensions of the task.

It's bad enough now. Even though the darkness helps, in that you keep your lamp trained on the space in front of you and rarely look up, you can still make out the dark outline of the mountain ahead of you and a few twinkling stars at the very top. You walk and you walk and you walk but the outline never changes, and the stars never move down one inch from the periphery of your vision.

Or perhaps the nighttime ascent has historic origins, and in that case we might have Hans Meyer to thank for setting the precedent. When he returned to Kilimanjaro for the third time in the year 1889, he eventually established a high-altitude camp at about 4,300 meters. The night before their planned summit attempt, he and his climbing partner Purtscheller were unable to sleep due to "the uncertainty of what the next day might bring forth." Ha! Don't I know it! Of course, my own uncertainty regarding summit night can't begin to compare to what these two pioneers must have felt, and once again I feel slightly ashamed of my fretting. But the sleeplessness I suffer from is exactly the same. Just like me they lay in their tent, and they "kept striking matches to see the time... every quarter of an hour," and finally, at 2:30 in the morning, they could stand it no longer and set out into the cold and pitch-dark night, "not a trace of the moonlight we had hoped for." I find the scene where Meyer takes leave of his faithful servant Mwini, who inexplicably slept between some rocks rather than in a tent, particularly moving:

"'Kwaheri' (good-bye), I called out to Mwini as I passed his cleft in the rocks. 'Kwaheri bwana na rudi salama'(good-bye, sir, and a safe return to you), was the answer. 'Inshallah' (if it be the will of God), I replied, and we stepped forth into the night."

They did not reach the summit that morning, because some unforeseen ravines bisecting what they thought was the most direct route slowed them down. "In the utter darkness it was desperately hard work," wrote Meyer, and even though their lanterns, "which were of Muscovy glass," sustained no damage, "the business of relighting them in the strong wind that was blowing tried our patience sadly."

When they finally reached the wall of ice marking the beginnings of the ice cap at 5,500 meters – which of course nowadays has receded almost completely – it was already mid-morning, and all they could do the rest of that day was cut steps into the ice ("each step cost some twenty strokes of the axe"), taking breaks every few minutes to double over and gasp for air. They did make it to the crater rim that day, October 3, where the sight of the "gigantic crater with precipitous walls, occupying the entire summit of the mountain" left them speechless, but from where they also could see that the actual summit was at least another hour and a half away. Faced with the danger of hypothermia, should they have to spend the night, they resolved to descend and return three days later to try to conquer the highest point.

So perhaps we are hiking at night simply because it's always been that way. Or perhaps it became tradition later on because it is such a joy to greet the rising sun from the summit. Or perhaps the true reason is based on necessity, because it is much easier, as well as safer, to scale the impossibly steep slope on frozen and therefore solid ground, whereas hours from now it will have turned into loose debris.

The night is clear and silent. We've started out with our headlamps on but realize after a while that the moonlight sufficiently lights the way. I smile as I recall the conversation months ago, the one in which I was so ignorant about the moon cycle. As it turns out, we've missed the full moon by a week or so, but it's still bright enough. Now I understand why seasoned Kili hikers place such importance on the phases of the moon. When we turn off our lamps, the mountain is instantly transformed. It is bathed in a soft glow, and we see the occasional twinkle of lights from groups ahead of us. The air is absolutely still and crisp, proving once again that it can always be worse – we could be in a storm, it could be snowing, we could be covered in sheets of ice, or we might have to extend 20 blows of an axe for each step.

I tell myself these comforting words, only I am so utterly cold. I feel a cold draft down my back and I've long lost all feeling in my fingers and toes. I can't even be bothered to wiggle them anymore. *So that's how it is with frostbite*, goes through my head. You always wonder how it can happen while you're in constant motion. But the more some parts of your body freeze, the less you move them, and eventually you give up altogether because it doesn't seem important anymore.

The reason my back is so cold, I discover at one of our rest stops, is that it's dripping wet. Somehow my Camelback insert is leaking, and I have water running out of my backpack. This is ironic, because the hose is frozen, so I cannot in fact drink any of the water that I am being so liberally doused with. And I can't get the leak fixed, because my fingers are too numb. Eventually, I just yank out the whole thing and dump the water out, attracting disbelieving stares from our guides who were diligently watching earlier to make sure we all took enough water. I probably couldn't have shocked them more if I had splashed the water directly in their faces. I immediately feel bad – after all, our porters have laboriously lugged this water up the mountain and here I'm acting as if I didn't appreciate it at all – but it does lighten my burden and gives me a chance to dry.

On we go again, in silence, one step at a time, each person focused on putting their foot into the print of the person before them. Someone described it like the passage of a funeral march, and the comparison is quite apt. We have fallen into a sort of slow-motion trot, one foot carefully in front of the other, turning left or right every few minutes to follow our zig-zag course because straight up is impossible. Going any faster would also be impossible, but curiously, going any slower is equally agonizing. As a result, each time you come upon a group of hikers walking even slower than you, you are faced with a decision: do we take the opportunity for a brief rest, or do we attempt to pass them? Aware that some of us are freezing, and trying to keep rests to a minimum, Goddy at times chooses to push on. But increasing our pace to get around the people in front of us requires a huge effort. On one occasion, when we take a brief rest, we see a group we just passed approaching again, and Goddy and Mike decide to get going before they pass us so as to avoid another passing maneuver later on. Unfortunately, the memo doesn't get handed down the line to Dylan and Martin who are still busy zipping up pants and rearranging loads, and they are temporarily left behind in the company of one of the assistant guides. Listening to their bitter complaints and tales of abandonment later, when they've caught up again, coupled with Mike's replies of "stop kaking on me already" (kak is an Afrikaans-derived South African slang word best translated as "crap") provides welcome comic relief for a short while.

We trudge on, and Max is complaining once more about being hot. Here I am shivering in my five layers, and he wants to take off his jacket! And still I hold my tongue, watching with concern as he is marching ahead of me wearing only his blue fleece. It's only when we come to another stop and lean against a rock in exhaustion that all hell breaks loose. One moment Max is standing next to me, asking me rather weakly to undo the buckles on his backpack so that he can take it off, and the next moment, while I'm bending down to fiddle once again with that cursed bladder, I hear a mighty clatter of poles banging against each other. I turn to the side and there is Max, lying next to me in a crumpled heap, quite lifeless.

Barafu Camp, September 7, about 10:00 AM

Only a few hours later, but a lifetime removed, I am reclining on a rock in front of our tent and resting my tired limbs. I glance behind me at the vast expanse above, and I shudder. I can't quite grasp that a mere half hour ago, I was still sliding and almost tumbling down that steep slope, Naiman – one of our guides – hot on my heels. Lance might have set a record for climbing Kili in 9 hours 45 minutes, but how about his descent back down? I'm quite sure that, in the world of Kili records, I created my very own this morning. Maybe not faster than Debbie Bachmann, she of the female Kili speed record from only a year ago. After she had conquered the summit and achieved her bid, she proceeded to run all the way down again, not so much because she wanted to set another record, but because she wanted to get back to her children. I feel a certain kinship with her. Maybe I can claim to be the fastest 40-something mother from Joburg between Uhuru and Barafu in 2012. I'm sure Naiman has never made the descent so fast either. It took us less than an hour to traverse what had taken over seven hours just a short while earlier in the other direction.

Max is stretched out on a rock right beside me, relaxing in the sunshine like a cat. There is no place I'd rather be than here, with him right next to me, safe and sound. I'm happy, and I feel great. It's as if a magic wand has passed over my body and taken all the pain and stress away. This is *my* Kili moment. For some it might be standing on top of the world that gives them the biggest satisfaction, but to me this moment is infinitely more gratifying. I feel at peace.

Everyone else is still somewhere up there, far above, and it is only now that I'm resting that I let my thoughts drift back to last night. I don't remember all the details of what happened after Max fainted, it all went so fast. I do remember not even finishing the thought "shit!" before several of our guides had already crowded around him, pushing out the others who were well-meaning but not well-trained, oxygen bottle in hand and slapping his face. He came to briefly, teeth clattering, then nodded off backwards again.

The most urgent problem seemed to be getting him warm, so I concentrated on one and one thing only, which was trying to put all those layers back on that he had shed, and more. Sharon found an extra fleece in her backpack that we were now frantically pulling over him. I was wrestling with one stray arm and uncooperative fingers while Hillary – was it Hillary? – was wrestling with the other, and when enough layers were on him, I managed to get more hand warmers ripped open and crammed into his gloves. There was a bit more yelling and shuffling and rapid Swahili flying between Hillary and Goddy, who had come back from up ahead to see what was going on, and before I could gather a coherent thought, I watched in disbelief as Max was carried off into the dark and down the mountain at a fast run on Hillary's and Peter's backs.

And I was not with him.

I'd like to say that I made a conscious decision for this to happen. That I would only have slowed them down, had I tried to follow. That those two guides knew best what he needed, and there was nothing I could contribute. That everyone knows that descending to a lower place is the perfect cure for altitude sickness – which this must have been, only with slightly different symptoms which I

now berate myself for not having paid closer attention to.
That had I followed at a slower pace, I would have needed
another guide, taking away precious manpower from the
rest of our group. That Max would have wanted me to
continue.

I'd like to say that I thought all those thoughts, but I
can't honestly say I did, at least not right then. One
moment he was there, and the next he wasn't, and I was
unable to make a quick enough decision, let alone gather
all my stuff that had been scattered around me in the
confusion. I do remember asking Goddy, whom I'd come
to trust with everything so far on the mountain, what they
were going to do and what I should do, and that he simply
said "you stay with us."

Once again, Goddy's word settled it, and this is how I
came to climb the rest of the long way to the summit
without Max, burdened with such a heavy heart I almost
couldn't bear it. I was convinced I'd done the wrong thing.
How could I not stay with my child? Even if he's 16 and
will cringe at being called a child when he reads this. The
wildest what-if scenarios were racing through my head. At
some point, I was convinced he would need to be
helicoptered off the mountain, and that the pilot would
refuse because I wasn't there with my credit card. It didn't
help that I later heard from others in our group that they
had talked through this very scenario beforehand and
made decisions on who would stay with whom or
continue to climb, should one of them have to turn
around. I had had no such conversations with Max –
another black mark on the mothering score sheet pointing
an accusing finger at my incompetence as a parent.

And then there was this tiny but nagging thought:
Had I really had no time to think it through, or had I
thought it through and made a split-second decision that I
didn't want to be stopped in my own quest to get to the
summit?

I don't think I'll ever know for sure. I do know that I had no joy in me the rest of the way, even if I did make it, somehow, up the mountain that long night, with all these second thoughts and doubts weighing on me heavily. At some point in time during another brief rest, Sharon, ever looking out for her charges and sensing I was struggling, told me to get out of the middle of the pack and right behind Goddy. "You'll be better off walking behind him," were her words, and she was right.

It's a funny thing. Some people are better to walk behind than others, one of the rather useless things you learn during a week of hiking on Kili. Unless you view it as a metaphor for going through life, and then it isn't useless at all. In any case, sticking to Goddy like a tick was what worked for me: not a wasted movement; his sure step; his calm confidence; and the singing. Oh, the singing!

I cannot quite adequately describe the feeling, but Goddy – sensing once again the exact moment when we needed it most, with another hour or so to go until Stella Point – began singing in his deep baritone, eliciting echoes from Naiman and Monday at the back of our line, letting the melody waft back and forth and ever so slowly up the mountain like an enchanted wave that carried us all along with it. "Soul-stirring stuff" is what Mike later called it. Dudley says he found "much more than irony" in the fact that at some point he had come to a stop, his willpower to take just one more step suddenly vanished, thinking "God help me!" and that at that precise point Godlisten responded and started singing. Goddy's name, which had struck us as such a good omen when we first met him, seems to have stood the test.

I only remember that it was like feeling extremely sad and happy at the same time. I'm not sure if we could have made it without the singing. I had tears streaming down my face, and yet I felt strengthened by it. There came a point where I knew I would make it, and from then on I couldn't get there fast enough. I just wanted to get there, take the picture, and turn around. The quickest way down to see how Max was doing, I realized, was leading right through the summit.

I know that in the years to come I'll be trying to recall the most unforgettable moments on the mountain, and that no matter how hard I try, some of them will have faded from memory, but the one moment I will never forget is when we finally reached Stella Point and crested the ridge overlooking the crater. I was so mindlessly following in Goddy's footsteps that I failed to notice he had stopped, and I was about to bump into him. He turned around and simply spread his arms open wide, and I stumbled into them, holding on for dear life and feeling as relieved as never before, thinking that now the end was in sight. And yet I think I was sobbing big, heaving sobs, unwilling to let go. All my sorrows seemed to flow out of me that instant and no one seemed to be able to understand me as well as Goddy. It can't have been long that we were standing there like that, and yet it felt like an eternity. I gathered a lot of strength from it, perhaps not just for the remaining distance to the summit, but for the rest of my life.

And then, shortly after six in the morning, came the sunrise, just as the last few climbers in our group had stumbled over the ridge and were still gasping for breath. I've seen many African sunrises and they've all been beautiful, but this has to have been the most captivating of all: standing on top of the world like this, overflowing with emotion, and wishing with all my heart for that little bit of warmth that for now was nothing more than a promise creeping over the horizon. The sun emerged slowly, seemingly floating up and out through the clouds against the panorama of Mawenzi's scraggly ridge, slowly turning the dull brown moonscape around us to fiery copper and casting long shadows behind us.

Stella Point is named after the wife of one of the early explorers. She is said to have stayed behind to rest while her husband forged on to the summit. At least that's what I think I read, but I cannot for the life of me find the passage again. Poor Stella seems to be mostly forgotten by history. Maybe she should have "pulled herself together" a little bit more and pushed on. But then again, she did get this splendid landmark named after her.

Even though no one wanted to stay in place very long on account of the cold, we used the opportunity to take our first real break after more than six hours of climbing, and after we'd all hugged and congratulated each other, we dropped down where we stood or remained standing, bent over our poles. For the first time since Barafu we could see in several directions. On one side was Mawenzi with the sun now floating above it, and on the other we had a magnificent view right into Reusch Crater, which in reality looks more like a large field of dark gray sand that is ringed by glaciers and ice fields around the edges. It is named after the Lutheran pastor Richard Reusch, the first to find a path down into it. In fact, I'll have to veer off topic again briefly on account of this amazing gentleman.

Richard Gustavovich Reusch was born into a German colony in Russia in the late 1800s, became a Cossack officer before changing careers and studying theology as well as Arabic, fought against the Bolsheviks, worked in Denmark as a private tutor, joined the British mission service in Tanganyika, climbed Kilimanjaro over 50 times, founded a mountain guide training program, served as a British spy while traveling throughout the region, published a bible in Swahili, became an expert on Islam, and befriended the Maasai, a fierce and independent tribe of warriors. It is also said that it was he who found the frozen body of a leopard right on the rim of Kibo's crater in 1926, which of course inspired Ernest Hemingway to write "Snows of Kilimanjaro" a few years later. I can't be sure if there is a connection to Reusch, the company, maker of gloves and other outdoor gear, but I wouldn't be surprised. Spending all this time in the arctic regions of Kilimanjaro would certainly have made him want to bring some warm mittens, and he sounds just like the kind of guy who would have started up his own brand in his spare time.

What's funny is how wildly our stories differ from this point on. Some in our group will tell you that the last bit from Stella Point to Uhuru Peak was pure agony and next to impossible to overcome. To me, it felt more like a walk in the park, at least once we were well on our way. While we were still getting ready to start walking again, so Mike told me later, I stood there with my face in my hands, sobbing inconsolably. I don't remember this. All I remember is that I was colder than I'd ever been in my life. Apparently I told Mike that all I wanted to do was go down again. He in turn told me that I couldn't, and that Uhuru was "right there." It seems only fitting that I not only owe the fact that I embarked on this trip to Mike and his relentless planning, but that it was he who ultimately pushed me over the last hurdle to make it to the top.

Maybe Mike gave his little pep talk as much to himself as to me, because he confided afterwards that the last stretch took all his remaining strength and every last bit of willpower. Dudley similarly thought he was done when we were about halfway between Stella and Uhuru. There was a small passageway the path led through, and he was thinking that Uhuru was just on the other side. When he realized how far it still was after he stepped around the bend, he remembered later, he sat down on a patch of scree, "angry with God or whoever it was that created this stupid fucking mountain." Only a few hundred meters from the summit, he all of a sudden felt quite happy to remain sitting there waiting for the others to come back down. Summiting just didn't seem important anymore. I'm not sure what changed his mind, and neither is he, but something prompted him to go on. Perhaps sometimes reminding ourselves that we do have a choice makes it easier to pick the harder one.

It's remarkable that everyone in our group did push on for the last bit. There are quite a few people who make it to Stella Point but not Uhuru, having spent their last ounce of energy to drag themselves over the crater rim and collapse, just like the Stella of yore. You can read story upon story about Kili climbers who had to turn around at Stella Point (or alternatively, if they were on the Marangu Route, Gillman's Point), so tantalizingly close to their goal but unable to go on.

As I said, what I remember is that it felt like a short walk, not nearly as steep as before and with the end point in plain sight – right over there and up a bit, just like Mike had told me. I'm not saying I sauntered up what was now a relatively gentle slope, but in hindsight it seems exactly like sauntering when contrasted with the agonizing crawl before Stella Point. All of a sudden, I felt new reserves of strength within me. It must have taken us another 45 minutes, and then we were there: At 6:53 AM on September 7, 2012, we stood on the roof of Africa. The entire continent was spread out at our feet. Finally, we had made it!

There were more hugs to go around, and more crying and sobbing fueled by all sorts of emotions everybody had carried along with them. It doesn't take much to make me cry – I was bawling my heart out as a new mother when I watched *The Lion King* for the first time – and God knows I had had enough to cry about throughout the night. But standing there on the summit, taking in 360 degrees of Africa all around us, I wasn't the only one crying. Dudley, who so shortly before was ready to give it all up, says that tears were not an option – they simply *had* to flow. Because what flooded him was the most incredible feeling of joy and achievement and sadness and exhaustion and gratitude and love all rolled into one.

I felt all of that, but the thing I most vividly remember is how very lonely I felt. Standing there on the summit of this mountain and at the end of my long road, I felt hollow. I was here, and yet the person I had most wanted to share this with, the person I had wanted next to me under that sign having our pictures snapped, was Max. Though I know he would have hated the picture taking part, and the fact that the picture would have to be taken again and again and again, each time with a different camera. He would have scoffed at such a waste of time ("why don't you people just trust each other and email the pictures afterwards?" had been his words a few days earlier) and he might have even refused to look into the camera. It brought to my mind our Christmas pictures of years past, the four grinning kids belying the almost epic battles often preceding that final snapshot: the stark refusals, the pouting, the yelling, the shoving, and the mounting pile of candy wrappers indisputable proof that we have, at times, indeed wielded that most potent parenting tool of all time – the bribe. I saw it all very clearly in my mind, and the thought almost made me smile.

Max wasn't in this for the glory. He wasn't in it to prove any point, or to tell anybody about it afterwards. He hates to be recognized for achievements. He'll go out of his way not to have to walk up on stage at school to receive any kind of award. He was only in it, from what I can tell, because I asked him to.

Which makes it all the more special to me that he came.

I've told you before how crowded the trek up Kili is. I've told you how it gets more crowded as you get closer to the top, after the different routes converge. So of course the very most crowded place is the top itself, and you practically have to stand in line to get a slot under the sign. It felt like we were lingering there forever, waiting our turn, even though it probably wasn't more than fifteen minutes. Some had plopped down wherever they came to a halt, grateful for the short reprieve for their weary legs, heads resting on backpacks and faces turned toward the slowly rising sun. I distinctly remember that I remained standing, as I had earlier at Stella Point, leaning onto my poles to gain back my breath. The thought of throwing myself on the ground did cross my mind, but I was quite certain that if I did, I'd never be able to get up again.

Somehow I managed to take a few pictures, despite my frozen fingers. My camera worked like a charm, even though I'd been warned that it might not, given these extreme temperatures. The only challenge was to pull it out of my backpack and turn it on. The glaciers, glinting in the morning sun, were particularly fascinating and provided a great backdrop. The huge walls of ice rising straight up ten meters and higher with their edges serrated as if cut with a giant's bread knife are only crippled remnants of what they once were, but nevertheless they are magnificent. When I stood up there in the bitter cold and saw all the ice around me, I couldn't imagine that it might ever melt away, as Monia had feared.

One of the glaciers is named after Dr. Walter Furtwängler who ascended Kilimanjaro in 1912 with the fourth group to summit and who was the first to ski down its slopes. Good thing he did it while he could, because nowadays there are no ski slopes left. Further afield I glimpsed what's referred to as the Northern Icefields, and beyond that another remnant of a glacier named after Johannes Rebmann, he who first described Kilimanjaro to fellow Europeans and was so widely scorned for his implausible tales of equatorial snow.

I admit I just love throwing around all these names of German explorers, the lot of them such esteemed gentlemen with their doctor's titles.

While we were waiting on the summit, paying close attention to the groups in front of us to make sure we wouldn't lose our spot in the queue, I had time to study the sign. It is made of several beams of light green metal,

all the same size and one on top of the other, the bright
yellow lettering proclaiming:

> **Congratulations!**
> **You are now at Uhuru Peak**
> **5895 M A.M.S.L.**
> **Tanzania**
> **Africa's highest point**
> **World's highest free standing mountain**
> **World heritage site**

Had we come just ten months earlier, we would still have
had the old wooden sign as our photo backdrop, the iconic
rather ragged-looking brown sign with faded lettering,
telling you the same facts as the new one but with so much
more style. For decades it had been the face of this
mountain for the entire world – even though the words
Kilimanjaro were not to be found on it – and now it was
gone. I felt a twinge of regret.

If you do the math, assuming that 35,000 people a
year attempt to summit Kilimanjaro, with about half of
those making it to the summit, you get about 50 climbers
taking their pictures next to the sign any given morning –
more if you count the guides, and a lot more if you give an
allowance for peak season. There were easily hundreds of
people who shared that space with us on the morning of
September 7, 2012. And they all brought cameras.

Meyer and Purtscheller, when they succeeded to
reach the summit on October 6, 1889, had it all to
themselves. They saw what no person had ever seen
before them: Mount Meru in the distance peeking out of
the clouds, the bright sunlight reflecting off the glaciers,
and off to the side the vast moonscape of ash or dark gray
sand with more ice fields beyond. All this was theirs and
theirs alone that moment in history, and you might think
they would have jumped and whooped with joy, but
according to Meyer all they did was shake hands, plant

the German flag, and name the place after the German emperor.

When it was finally our turn, we scrambled to shuffle into place. A South African flag someone had had the presence of mind to bring along materialized, and just as Max might have predicted we had our group shot taken by a kindly soul from one of the groups trailing us who didn't seem to mind repeating it with every camera we handed him. Then there were shots of smaller groups, followed by some of us all by ourselves. I got no joy from that exercise, and I'll forever loathe the picture of me leaning against the sign in what should have been such a victorious pose. All I could think of at that moment was how desperately I wanted to get down again. Mainly to get back to Max and see with my own eyes that he was fine, but also out of a sense of self-preservation. Even with the sun now shining brightly, the temperature was still far below freezing. I almost couldn't feel the cold anymore, but I knew that for the sake of my frozen extremities I had to get down to milder regions as soon as possible.

I was the first to be off. It must have been at around 7:25 AM, judging by the time stamps on my summit pictures. I had spent about half an hour on the summit, and it had felt like an eternity. Naiman – and I will always be grateful for this – recognized that I wanted to get down fast and stayed with me the whole way. The two of us were flying down that mountain. The closest I can come to describing how it felt is the way you ski down a black diamond slope around moguls. Not that I'm very good on black diamond slopes, mind you. It was more what skiing down a black diamond slope *would* feel like, if I could do it well. I had relied on my hiking poles before, but I absolutely came to love them then. Without them it wouldn't have been nearly as fast, or – I admit – fun. I'd plant the poles far in front of me, hop down, and slide about another meter in the deep scree, a big cloud of dust billowing up around me, then plant the poles again, and so on, all the way down, always careful to navigate around large rocks.

I might have been even faster had Naiman not sat me down every once in a while and forced me to drink what was left of my water. I'm glad he did, as it gave me time to snap a few pictures and admire the view, which was spectacular. Without the biting cold at the summit I was able to relish it even more. The clouds had lifted and I could see, far below, the little colored dots of Barafu Camp where it stood on an outcropping almost close enough to touch in the crisp air, and beyond it the rest of the mountain and the steppes below, all of it distorted by the curvature of the Earth.

After just five minutes of this, my toes and hands were thoroughly thawed and pulsing with circulation, and it didn't take long before the first layers of clothes had to come off. Occasionally we'd encounter a climber and his guide who were still making their slow ascent, huddled under their balaclavas and hoods and looking miserable, and they must have stared at my sauntering t-shirt-clad self in disbelief, if not disgust. The contrast was almost laughable. Just an hour earlier I had looked and felt exactly like that, and now here I was free as a bird and having a grand old time, fueled by my eagerness to see my son again soon.

Completely breathless and unable to utter a word, I tumbled through the tent flap a short while later when I arrived back in camp. I laughed and cried from relief when I was finally able to put my arms around Max. He was contentedly sitting on his sleeping bag and assured me that he was fine. He had gotten a good night's sleep after a long drink of water once back in his tent, and Hillary had temporarily moved in with him to watch him closely and make sure he was alright – a side note that endears all of Goddy's team even more to me.

If there was any disappointment within Max, now that he was feeling well again, he hid it well. He bears no physical scars, though I can't even begin to imagine the emotions he must have coped with last night once he was able to think clearly again, grappling with the fact that he didn't make it when everyone else did. I'm sure this will bother him. Perhaps it will confirm his belief that it's best to only try out those things that promise near certain success. Because who wants failure? Who wants disappointment, missed goals, or unfulfilled hope? But perhaps this experience will teach him that success and failure go together like day and night. That one hardly stands out without the other. That each time we fail a tiny door opens into the future, and if we can only find it and step through it, there is nothing we can't one day achieve in life.

Perhaps Max can find comfort in the example of Thomas Edison. When Edison invented the light bulb, he was thwarted by countless failed tries. Every time he'd come up with a new approach, he'd run into yet another dead end, again and again and again. Had he subscribed to the more common definition of failure, perhaps we'd still be sitting in dim rooms breathing in petroleum fumes. But he just kept on going. When asked about it, he is reported to have said something akin to: "I have not failed. I've just found 10,000 ways that won't work."

I hope that this is the lesson Max will take home from our adventure. Indeed, he says he is quite certain that he will be back to try it again.

Who knows, I might even go with him.

Sunrise over Stella Point

Day Seven: Down, Down, Down, and Straight to the Bar

Barafu Camp to Mweka Camp to Machame Gate, Sep 7 and Sep 8, 2012
Distance: 12-13 km, 6-7 hours to Mweka Camp and 10 km, 3 hours to Machame Gate
Elevation: 1,600 m descent from Barafu to Mweka Camp at 3,000 m and 1,200 m descent from Mweka Camp to Machame Gate at 1,800 m.

The seventh day, technically speaking, also begins on the previous day, which is where we find ourselves now, on the late morning of Day Six. It's hard to believe that it's still only morning when so much has already happened on this day, even though the longest part of it is still to come.

We rest at Barafu Camp for a few hours, once the remaining members of our group have returned, and have lunch there one last time. It takes quite an effort to summon enough energy to pack up our belongings, but we need to make room for the newly arriving groups. The weather, so sunny less than an hour ago, has turned, and for the first time on the mountain we experience snowfall. Not a heavy one, to be sure, but enough to leave a white dusting on the mess tent and to spur us on to our downward trek.

Mweka Camp is another 13 kilometers or so away, meaning six or seven hours of walking, perhaps more. The Mweka Route, as I've already mentioned, is only used for

the descent, so from now on we won't encounter any
climbers going the other way. We soon break up into
smaller groups – those going fast and those taking a
slower, more careful approach to go easy on their knees.

It proves to be a long hike. Granted, it is all downhill
and therefore not nearly as strenuous as what we've done
earlier today, and yet I am eagerly awaiting our arrival at
the next camp. We've barely slept in the last 24 hours and
it is beginning to show. I feel as though I'm only walking
so tirelessly because gravity pulls me downward, as if
stopping would require an even bigger effort. Even so, it's
amazing how fast we advance. Imagine our ascent as a
movie, for a moment, and then think of someone
rewinding it at five times the speed. That is the best way to
describe our downward hike.

While I carefully step around boulders on my way
downwards, I absently finger a small rock in my pocket. I
picked it up at the summit while we were waiting for our
turn to take pictures under the sign, and it now brings
back a memory that makes me smile. It was still early on,
maybe our first or second day on the mountain, and we
were resting on an outcropping of rocks to eat lunch. I was
sitting there admiring the view when Mike walked up to
me, straining under the weight of a huge boulder he could
barely lift.

"Here," he said, laid the rock down carefully at my
feet, and turned around.

"What?" I asked, wondering if the sun had beaten
down on him too much.

"It's your rock," he said. "You told me you wanted to
bring home a rock from Kilimanjaro."

It was such a brief moment, and yet it epitomizes the
experience of camaraderie we've had this last week.
Without people making silly jokes, it wouldn't have been
half as fun. I also find it endearing that Mike remembered
such an offhand remark of mine.

I wonder what I should do with the little rock in my pocket when I get home. Hans Meyer, who of course also picked up a few rocks from Kibo's slopes, never had a doubt. When he finally returned to Germany after his expedition, he "was called upon to give my report to the Emperor, and his Majesty was graciously pleased to accept at my hands the topmost pinnacle of the Kaiser Wilhelm's Peak, which I had not forgotten to bring along with me in my pocket." The rocks were later built into the grotto hall of the emperor's residence in Potsdam, the marble palace, where they still grace the wall to this day. Or, rather, *some* kind of volcanic rock graces the wall, but it is now suspected to be a fake. Nobody seems to know how or when the original specimen was stolen and what became of it, and digging in old records to determine its fate would make for an intriguing subject for another book.

I doubt anyone in Johannesburg will care that much about *my* rock. I was neither the first to summit, nor am I acquainted with any emperors. I guess I'll put it somewhere on my bookshelf, where it will serve to remind me of my adventure from time to time.

When we finally stop for a brief rest, an interesting contraption leaning against a rock catches our eye. It looks like a steel gurney with large grips on either end and a fat bicycle wheel on shock absorbers mounted under it.

"Kilimanjaro ambulance," says Goddy offhandedly and moves on. So this is how you get off the mountain if you can't walk on your own feet, we realize. You are carried down the steepest parts on someone's back, and if you still need further evacuation, you are strapped to one of these things and maneuvered – on what I can only imagine is a brutal trip for both you and the porters pushing the thing – all the way to a place like Shira where a helicopter can land to evacuate you if necessary. I shudder at the thought and once again say a silent prayer of thanks that Max was spared that ordeal. What he isn't spared now, however, is the ordeal of having to sit on the "ambulance" and having his picture taken while Martin and Mike direct the scene. It's a sign of how much he has grown this past week that he's tolerating it all like a good sport, a big grin on his face.

When finally, one after the other, we trickle into camp in the late afternoon, we collapse onto some chairs in front of the mess tent. We are utterly exhausted but in high spirits. We gratefully sip some warm Cokes and beers that have magically appeared, and we laugh out loud once we get a good look at one another. We're a sight to behold. The men are all unshaven, of course, everyone's hair emerging from under their beanies is a matted tangle, and we are covered in dust from head to toe. We must look absolutely revolting, and God knows what we smell like, but no one cares. In fact, everyone seems to have an almost radiant glow about them which I, for one, find oddly attractive.

Mike is in his element telling the first battle stories, and it almost feels like the beginning of a slightly premature post-climb party, but all too soon the gathering breaks up and we repair to our various tents. It's not over yet, and we've all got odds and ends to attend to. Since this is our last camp on the mountain, it's time to clean house and make sure nothing gets left behind. Sleeping bags are aired, sweat-soaked t-shirts are hung out to dry, ACE packs are applied to swollen knees, and massages are given to knotted shoulders and blistered feet. The whole place has the feel of an army camp during a lull in battle. I make an attempt at ridding my body of those thick layers of soot I gathered while skating down from Uhuru, but other than turning my bowl of washing water to instant brown, this hardly makes a difference.

By the time we finish dinner, our energy has dissipated and the mood shifted. Most likely because we are incredibly exhausted after the exertions of the last two days, but, I suspect, also because a certain melancholy has set in. Tonight is the last time we're sharing this now so familiar routine: the last pot of soup we're dipping the ladle into; the last time we wait with baited breath to see who gets the broken chair and suddenly sags off to the side mid-sentence; the last time Goddy quizzes us on all the Swahili phrases he's been teaching us; the last time we sleep in the shadow of this awesome mountain.

Out of pure habit I pull the hood of my sleeping bag tight around my face when we settle down, but I pay dearly for it later at night. Even though we are still at 3,000 meters altitude, the night feels positively tropical in comparison to the last few ones. I wake up soaked in sweat from all the trapped heat and am immediately wide awake. Maybe waking up in the middle of the night has become a habit in and of itself. I go and pay a last nighttime visit to Tee-Tee for old times' sake and discover that once again there is a line. I'm not the only one haunted by sleeplessness.

There's so much to think about. Only now does what we've done today truly begin to sink into my mind, and I lie there for hours, alone with my thoughts and unable to sleep.

The next morning we rise early, say a final good-bye to our tents as they are packed up, and are treated to another serenade of the "Kili Song" by all the porters and guides. It's a heartwarming sight, all of them lined up in the early-morning mist and giving us this last dance, some of them proudly donning discarded boots and hats they've been given. Though not *my* boots, nor Max's. Even though we've had no more words about it, this is perhaps the first sign that deep down neither of us has completely closed this chapter.

We try to soak up every word from *Jambo, bwana* onwards, knowing we will want to recall this moment in the months to come, and then we begin the last descent to the park gate, scattering again into small groups. Even though it's a relatively short hike, as opposed to everything we've done before, it isn't easy to negotiate.

Once again the path resembles a giant staircase hewn into the slope, with wooden planks demarking the sides and edges of each step, all of them worn smooth over the years of traffic. A recent rain has rendered the path extremely muddy and the wood extremely slippery so that staying upright and avoiding the indignity of a soggy bottom proves quite the challenge.

I can also feel the beginning of a blister starting on my big toe. After all the care I've taken with double layers of socks, which worked quite well going up the mountain, the repeated ramming of my toes into the front of the boots during the long descent is taking its toll. The poles are a big help, however – indispensable, in fact, especially in these soggy conditions – and I thank the stars that I did take that particular piece of advice to heart.

I hang out with the boys for a while, and they are practically jogging down the mountain. It's quite the challenge to keep up, but it's a challenge I enjoy. You have to concentrate on the path, make quick decisions where to plant your pole, and take big leaps to jump down each step. Once again, this reminds me of skiing down a slope covered in moguls. Hillary, who I think has developed a feeling of protective affection for Max through their shared experience, is also with us. It is he who stops us in our tracks midway down and leads us a few steps off the path to show us something special. There, through a clearing framed by tropical trees, is Kibo in its glorious splendor, glinting in the bright sunshine under a deep blue sky and covered in what looks like freshly-fallen snow. *Kilima njaro,* Shining Hills: It really is a fitting name. This is possibly the best view of Kilimanjaro we've had yet, and only reluctantly can we tear ourselves away and resume our descent. When I turn around a few minutes later to catch another glimpse, Kibo is gone, obscured once again by the dense forest and the formation of midday clouds. It's almost as if we imagined the whole thing.

When we arrive at the park gate just a few hours later, it feels like a let-down. We can't possibly be done, can we? We linger some more, sign our names into the log book one last time, and buy the "Been there, done that" t-shirts and Kili bracelets and other tacky souvenirs we were told to bring some cash for. But then the moment arrives when it's time to climb into the old military truck that is waiting to take us back to the hotel and to declare our adventure finished. Contrary to what I might have thought months earlier, when the prospect of walking every single day seemed daunting, I now feel that reclining in a seat to be whisked to a distant place in relative comfort is unsatisfying. It feels as if we're cheated out of something by not walking on our own two feet. We all sit in silence as we bump along, small villages and coffee plantations passing by outside the windows and people waving at us occasionally, their lives going on as before.

For us, nothing seems the same as before. In seven days, we have climbed up 4,000 meters and down again – 6,200 meters if you count all the valley traverses on the way up. We've hiked a total of about 70 kilometers. A bit more for Mike, on account of his hat. We've endured temperatures far below freezing and oxygen concentrations far thinner than what seems possible. We've had to contend with all the discomforts of living in the great outdoors, albeit greatly tempered thanks to the small daily luxuries provided by our crew. All of this has had an impact on us, but not just a physical one. Dudley, I think, has summarized it best. Climbing Kilimanjaro, he says, "gives you a completely new appreciation of life and the meaning of a journey well-traveled. A tour de force and a tour of friendships newly won."

And now our tour is nearing its end.

No one feels like talking on this last piece of our journey; everyone is lost in their own thoughts. Mine drift back to the last two days. I haven't taken notes since the free afternoon we had at Barafu when we were anxiously anticipating our push for the summit, and so much has happened since then. There was summit night and all its drama, of course, but now I compel myself to recall the descent, lest my memories of it get lost among the other highlights of last week.

Hiking down Kilimanjaro happened so fast that it was a blur. Some of us flew down on wings we didn't know we had, gaining energy with every oxygen-loaded breath we inhaled, while some of us took a bit longer, slowed down by a few uncooperative knees. The scenery was flying by so fast that one minute you found yourself sliding down a field of crushed rocks where nothing grows, and the next you were surrounded by dense and foggy rain forest, not quite remembering how you got from here to there. The descent would have been the time for frequent stops to take pictures and soak in the last of the atmosphere, but when I check my camera – which I'm startled to find still has three bars of battery left – I see that I have a total of three images from the downward hike.

Looking back, it's hard to understand the rush, but at the time it felt as if gravity increased with each step and inexorably pulled you downhill as if you were on autopilot. You remember coming through all of it in reverse just days ago, and the contrast is so stark it makes you laugh. You think back to how your group crawled uphill, and how you had your gaze fixed mostly on the square meter of ground in front of you. You recall how you stared at the garden trowel dangling from the preceding backpack, giving you endless hours of contemplation of where it might have been and what it might or might not have touched. You revive these images while down, down, down you go, and when you think there can't be any more mountain left, you go down some more.

Perhaps what also pulls you toward the bottom at such speed is the idea that you'll soon see your family again. I can understand what prompted Debbie Bachmann to run down the mountain more or less nonstop, even though she had already achieved her record and might have wanted to linger, to revel in it longer. Although this adventure belongs to Max and me, and although I've greatly enjoyed leaving my day job of housewife and mother behind, I do miss the other kids, as well as Klaus. In his case I'll have to wait a little longer for a face-to-face reunion on account of the new job he has just started in the United States, a long way removed from Johannesburg. But my reunion with our three younger kids is just a day away.

Or perhaps the sole reason you're running down the mountain so fast is simply because you can.

I consciously tried to slow myself down on the last stretch. I wanted to delay the inevitable end, and I enjoyed having time for the conversations we couldn't have before, when we were always gasping for breath. I can't recall what we talked about – gone were the existential questions of eggs and vacuums – but I enjoyed the banter. Although what seemed like banter to me might have been grunts through gritted teeth by others. I know I'm not being fair to some in our group by my portrayal of a carefree downhill hike. I did have to watch where I stepped, and it was an exercise in concentration, but it was one I enjoyed.

If you had knee problems, on the other hand, it was agony. Dudley and Adrian had an especially hard time going down, gingerly stepping around boulders and trying to get a foothold on the slippery mud, faces drawn with pain. It must have been frustrating being passed by everyone else, and both of them maintain that they would gladly have swapped another summit night for the downhill bit.

As you get closer to the bottom, you start thinking about the hotel awaiting you, and you allow yourself to daydream about that long-awaited shower as well as simpler long-awaited pleasures. Yes, I'm talking of getting to the toilet at night without any pesky zippers standing between you and a good dump, and sitting on said toilet separated from the rest of the world by solid walls rather than thin canvas that might blow away any moment; and, while we're at it, sitting on your seat with the comforting knowledge that it is affixed to the ground in a level position in no immediate danger of toppling over with you on it.

Of one thing I'm sure: I never thought I would one day write this much about toilets. Or garden trowels.

And yet, as much as you look forward to the comforts of civilization, each step that takes you closer to them makes you sadder. Because you realize that something very special is coming to an end. I find that it feels a little bit like coming home from my first class trip as a teenager: I've grown very close to my group, we break out in giggles at the mere mention of a shared experience, and I fondly remember all the food, even if they didn't exactly serve us five-star meals. We've spent a week on one long amazing high and now we go home filthy, happy, and sad all at the same time, quite sure that people who didn't have the experience will never understand.

But we're not quite there yet. Because which good hiking trip ends without a few cold drinks afterwards?

It is said that you can easily distinguish South Africans from Americans when returning from their Kili climb: the former will always head straight to the bar for a round of ice cold Kilimanjaro beers, while the latter go straight to the shower, or so the legend goes. It must be a testament to my having one foot firmly planted on each continent that once we have spilled out of the truck back at our hotel, I find myself stranded at a crossroads on the gravel path, unable to move. I am called from one direction by my American son who is desperate to get a room – with the goal, no doubt, to take the longest shower of his life – and from the other direction by my South African friends to come have my first beer out in the courtyard with the rest of our crew. I stand there rooted to the spot for a few long moments, not knowing what to do. In the end, Max gets the shower and I the beer, followed by many glasses of wine and, as the night progresses, champagne.

Quite honestly, I would've been happy with a few liters of vegetable juice as long as it was cold and didn't taste of chlorine, but I won't say I'm not enjoying the alcohol. I'm perfectly happy to sit here in the warm sunshine for hours in my filthy outfit and bare feet amidst this group of dear friends. It seems I am well on my way to becoming a true South African at heart just as we're getting ready to leave this country again. It's the story of our lives – that we are forever leaving places right at the moment we've fallen in love with them and are thinking of putting down roots.

Figuring out the tip schedule for the porters and guides is quite the exercise, and one I can highly recommend having completed before too many beers have been consumed. I can also advise you, should you contemplate a Kili climb, to bring about twice as many US dollars as you originally calculated so meticulously. Because you will happily spend a small fortune on the aforementioned t-shirts and other mementos; because you might need some extra cash to pay some ridiculous departure fees at the airport that no one told you about; and because you will want to be very generous to the people who have so little and yet gave so freely of everything they could offer to ensure your well-being that week. Just remember: Some of them might have carried you down a mountain on their backs.

Nothing qualifies you so well to dispense helpful advice as when you haven't followed it yourself. Because of course I *haven't* brought enough dollars. As Klaus will be quick to tell you, I don't concern myself with such pesky details as much as I should, and so I find myself squeezed into the backseat of Hillary's car on another adventure before the current one has been duly celebrated. Martin and Adrian, who are similarly short of cash (and similarly lacking in foresight, I take comfort in noticing), are on either side of me, all of us still giggling from our first round of beers and now bumping through dusty Moshi in search of an ATM. I haven't brought my camera, but the sights are almost as inviting as earlier on the mountain, like the guy balancing an entire pallet of firewood on his bicycle. Once more it feels strange not to do this errand on foot, and stranger still to see our trusted guide transformed into a driver.

Amazingly, the first bank machine we stop at happily spits out hundreds of thousands of Tanzanian shillings for all our various cards, and then it willingly gives some more after we've reached the transaction limit and insert our cards a second time. I know I should be suspicious of what amounts of fees might materialize on our next bank statement, and I'm not sure if our altitude- and alcohol-addled brains have gotten even close to the correct exchange rate, but nothing is going to detract from our happiness today.

Upon our return to the hotel, the money is duly handed over to Mike, who has installed himself under an umbrella in the courtyard and has volunteered for the thankless task of counting it and figuring out who gets what. He performs what seems a miracle of mathematical wizardry, helped along by another round of beers, and finally hands varying stacks of bills to Goddy, Hillary, Naiman, and Monday, who graciously accept what likely amounts to the highlight of their week. We also hand Goddy a tip schedule so that he can give everyone else not present their share.

Next the tables are turned and we find ourselves on the receiving end. Goddy calls us up one by one, gives a little speech, and hands out our certificates, followed by pictures with the guides shaking our hands and a round of applause. When it is Max's turn, he is hoisted into the air by Goddy and Hillary for a special photo op, and again he good-naturedly endures being singled out in this way. He may not have made his way to the very top of the mountain, but he certainly made it all the way into the hearts of these two guys.

Eventually the moment arrives when we have to part, and our guides take their leave from us after many rounds of well-wishing in every direction. No doubt they are eager to get back to their homes and their families and the task of organizing their daily lives. I just hope that this time they get more than a day's rest before the next group arrives.

It isn't quite as hard to say good-bye to Goddy as I have imagined, because due to a fortunate coincidence he will be traveling to South Africa soon. Some former climbers have banded together and financed a trip for him to visit Johannesburg in exactly one month. It is to be his first journey ever beyond the borders of Tanzania, and he can't help grinning about it from ear to ear. We know we'll see him again soon.

Even so, it is an emotional good-bye, perhaps more on our part than on Goddy's, as surely he must be used to these scenes after years of guiding groups up the mountain. You can't help but grow close to your guide who has accompanied or rather led you through seven such meaningful days of your life. I do, however, think that Goddy has grown very fond of us too. There were several occasions when he confided how touched he was that we treated him like a "someone" when he was such a "nobody." Those were his words, not ours. He couldn't imagine that, to us, he was everything. He was the one we turned to for advice, he was the one who cheered us up when we were down, he was the one who inspired us to dig deeper and find our inner reserves of strength.

It is sad to think that apparently some climbers do not see the same in their guides, or else Goddy wouldn't feel that way. He was almost in tears the one evening we emptied our collective medical kits to dig for painkillers for one of the porters who suffered from a toothache and needed to go off the mountain. Goddy couldn't believe that we helped a "lowly" porter, even though it was such a small gesture on our part.

I will never forget Kilimanjaro, and I will never forget Godlisten Mkonyi.

In what I know to be a blend of African languages: *Hamba kahle kaka yangu.*

Go well, my brother.

Remaining glaciers on the summit of Kilimanjaro

Day Eight: Departure

September 9, 2012, departure to Johannesburg

I always like the act of packing up for a return trip much more than its counterpart at the beginning of a journey, even though I suspect for most people it is the opposite. Perhaps this stems from my perpetual indecision, but I just love throwing everything into a bag without regard for organization and without any decisions to make, because whatever you brought has to go back home. I never need much time for it at all.

But when I sat in our room yesterday afternoon, after Goddy's departure and before dinner, I took my time. While I unpacked our duffel bags and sorted through the results of living outdoors for a week, I recalled how painstakingly I had packed in preparation for this trip. I knew how unceremoniously I was going to dump it all out back home, so I decided to proceed slowly and carefully look at everything to reflect on which of these items I had most come to rely on during our trek.

I already mentioned the hiking poles. I had rented mine and Max's for a very reasonable amount right here at the hotel. I fretted quite a bit over whether to get them or not, prior to our trip, and now I know they were absolutely essential, both for summit night and for the entire descent. At the very least, they were useful for banging people over the head whose cellphone was beeping while you were trying to take a nap.

The wet wipes deserve another mention here, even though I had to recall them from memory because every single one was gone. Why I hadn't just brought an extra pack, I don't know. Like I said, I sometimes follow directions too slavishly, and I don't think the wet wipes made an appearance on any of my packing lists. They're not biodegradable, that's true, but seeing as our other trash had to be taken down the mountain anyway, a few wet wipes more or less wouldn't have made a dent at all. I'm probably just not American enough. Most American women I know don't go anywhere without a gigantic pack of wet wipes.

The same goes for toilet paper. And enough said about *that* topic.

The headlamps I bought were not the cheapest kind but good-quality ones and long-lasting. They were definitely a smart investment, and I would take them again, even without any nighttime hikes. It's so much easier to find your way around your tent and bag with the lamp attached to your head rather than clamping it between your teeth. Toward the end of the week, I took to sleeping with it tightly wrapped around my wrist.

I didn't need them but would still bring them again: extra batteries for the headlamp.

Remember all my fretting over the microfiber towel when shopping for supplies? Well, I did end up buying one (a blue one, in case you want to know) and I must say I liked having it to dry my hands and face after washing. Also, it was very easy to dry by hanging it from the dome of the tent by night and from the zipper of my backpack by day. I should mention that I originally bought two towels and gave one to Max for his school hiking trip in March, which it never made it back from, although he maintains that he didn't lose it. He just "didn't know where it was." So we had to share the one towel, and it rendered good service. Although, quite frankly, a microfiber cleaning rag from my laundry room would have done just as nicely and cost me nothing. You definitely don't need anything of bath towel dimensions; because I can promise you that there won't be a single shower on all of Kilimanjaro.

The one item I only used on the first day, and didn't even need then, was the pair of gaiters, those long tubes made from a sturdy material that you pull over the top of your boots to keep out rain and snow and mud. We had neither rain nor snow nor mud (or at least not enough to make a difference), but I'd bring them again because you never know.

I already mentioned the special relationship I had with my beanie. I wore it every day (and most every night). They say that most of your body heat departs through your head, but through years and years of skiing I have never found that to be true for me. Maybe I have too much hair for that effect. I definitely needed it for summit night, but when I highly recommend bringing a beanie along – especially one that's not scratchy – I do it not so much in view of protection from the elements but in view of covering up your unwashed hair.

How did I rate my fancy socks, you wonder? They were absolutely perfect, delivering as much as promised. I took special pleasure from fishing them out of my bag each morning and inspecting them for the bright red "L" and "R" to help me decide which one went on which foot. I took great care not to mix them up, mainly because after several days they were molded into the precise shape of my toes, but perhaps also out of some superstitious streak I did not know I had. That mountain has a pull on you in many ways.

The boots deserve some credit too. I never came to resent them in any way, as you so often hear in other hiking stories. I never felt any loathing while lacing them up each morning, and it was almost with something akin to regret that I stepped out of them for the last time.

The other thing I absolutely came to love is my self-inflating pillow. They don't show up on many packing lists because they're not considered essential, but it made a big difference during my – admittedly mostly sleepless – nights. They're not expensive and can be rolled tight into practically nothing, so there's no big downside to bringing one along. There's only the upside of lying more comfortably while not sleeping.

I didn't take my mobile phone on the hike. Without an international plan it was practically useless, and it would have run out of battery after two days at most. But I was able to get some messages off to Klaus via a borrowed phone and know that he has absolutely loved hearing from us in this way. Okay, not just any borrowed phone, I'll admit, but Adrian's phone limping along with the help of the beeping charger we all cursed so much. So I want to give it (and Adrian) some credit here. If I were to do it again, I would buy a cheap prepaid phone with some international minutes and use it very sparingly for a few text messages here and there. Although Klaus will be the first to say that the words "mobile phone" and "use sparingly" are not often found together in any sentence describing me.

There isn't much more left to say. My Kili adventure is coming to an end, and so is my tale. There is also not much left to say because, ahem, my memory is a bit hazy about last night. After I had unpacked, I joined the others in the courtyard to resume our rounds of beer after the late afternoon break in our rooms, and we ended up getting really drunk. We derived a lot of enjoyment from laughing about the same jokes over and over again, and, in a sudden spurt of creativity, coming up with everyone's alias for my upcoming blog posts. It was the sort of creative frenzy you can only summon when you've just come off a mountain together and shared one too many rounds of Kilimanjaro beers in the aftermath to expunge forever the lingering taste of seven days' worth of water purification tablets.

I've already told you that we christened Mike the Fat Controller for his propensity to direct everyone around. Martin became Woody, the connection escaping me now, but it seemed outrageously funny in that courtyard yesterday, empty bottles heaped around us. Dudley became Johnny Fartpants, a cartoon character I was not familiar with until then but the connection of which escapes no one, as I'm sure it didn't escape Sharon, his sleeping bag partner. Sharon herself became Bo-Peep, getting her nickname from the bright pink floppy hat that always shone like a beacon to lead the way. Adrian became Professor Calculus, who – as you might recall if like me you've spent your childhood reading every single book in the *Tintin* series – always brings along one of his new scientific discoveries which unfortunately often don't work quite as expected. So it was with Adrian's home-fashioned solar cellphone charger, the one we never ceased to tease him about. David was named Mr. Potato Head, due to his habit of breaking stuff and then relying on Adrian to put it all back together again.

I know all this sounds pretty ridiculous and childish, but once we got going there was no stopping us. And you also have to know that assigning nicknames is an African thing. Everybody gets one, and typically those names are very clever. I take comfort in the fact that even the honorable Hans Meyer, conqueror of Kilimanjaro, was answering to a rather silly pseudonym his Somali and African porters had assigned him during their joint travels: Bwana kelele (Mr. Silence). Here is what he has to say about how he got that name:

"...when retiring for the night, we were often much annoyed by the noise made by the men outside as they sat laughing and chattering around the fires. On these occasions I used to give vent to my feelings and order them off to bed with an imperious *kelele*; hence my title of "Bwana kelele.'"

Somehow this little story endears Meyer even more to me, because once again I feel as if we are kindred spirits. If my kids were giving out nicknames at our house, "Missus Silence" is very well one I might get stuck with.

Silence, by contrast, is not something Dylan practices often. He loves to talk, and not only that, he can do it in many cool accents. Which is why in our naming session he became Sebastian the crab, from *Ariel*. His imitation of OR Tambo International Airport announcers broadcasting flight details and inadvertently discussing their order of fried chicken on the open mic had us rolling on the floor laughing several times. Monia inevitably had to be Dory from *Finding Nemo*, as she was always talking and asking so many questions (and, because like Dory, she has a heart of gold). I myself became Olive, woman friend of Popeye, which I flatter myself must surely be related to Olive's girlish figure. Only Max was spared a new nickname, considering he already has one. In fact, maybe he deserves to be rid of that one forever. Because for these past ten days he hasn't been a stubborn Zax at all.

I think I remember that in the midst of all our joking and celebrating the guys invited a solo-hiking Scandinavian girl named Ingrid – young, blond, and slender – to share drinks with us as the evening progressed, and that all of them seemed eager to vie for her attention by telling her the most fantastical stories about our climb. But I could be wrong. I'm almost certain there wasn't any tall gorgeous male equivalent named Bjorn to give massages to all the women in our group, and I also don't recall Lance stopping in for another visit in his skin-tight shirt, a rough stubble accentuating his handsome features. But again my memory might fail me. Who is to say? I sometimes wonder which parts of our week were fantasy and which ones were true. You'd have to ask the boys what truly happened that last evening, but given the fact that we possibly slipped them a few beers and insisted that they drink up, you might not have much luck there either.

The hotel staff had to practically kick us out of our chairs when the place closed down for the night, and then there were a few hiccups when we wanted to settle our bills and the credit card machine wasn't working. But somehow it got taken care of to everyone's satisfaction, and we all staggered to our rooms to fall into bed and a very exhausted sleep. Or almost all of us, I should say. Still haunted by sleeplessness, I spent part of the short night draped on a sofa in the lobby, writing up the beginnings of this story.

Oh, and that shower did indeed feel wonderful. I'll turn to Dr. Hans Meyer one more time who got it quite right when he wrote: "At home all these things [like cigars and coffee after lunch, or the trifling over the pages of an illustrated paper] are commonplace enough, we take them as a matter of course. Roughing it in a country like East Africa is the surest way to teach us the true value of our little comforts, and we first discover how much we appreciate them when we think we have begun to learn to do without them."

I feel that at times he truly read my future mind when he penned his story some 120-odd years ago. I will never forget what a sheer pleasure and privilege running warm water is. I almost cried from joy when I rubbed the first drop of shampoo into my hair. Or rather a whole bottle, if I'm completely honest. And I most definitely cried when I stood there, steaming water cascading down on me, and thought back to the incredible week I'd just had.

It seems fitting to close my story with what my American friend Phil, who summited independently of our group just a week before us, told me after his return about his shower experience:

For the last hour of the descent I was daydreaming about my shower back at the lodge. However, once we got there, I got into the shower only to discover that the lodge was totally, and I mean TOTALLY, out of hot water. Brutal. Then, to add to the experience, I realized I had no soap. So as I was standing there in my filth getting soaked with freezing cold water, feeling a little sorry for myself, I asked what else could go wrong. At that moment the power went out, so my glorious hot shower was now a soft trickle of freezing water in pitch darkness. This is Africa!

It all got sorted out in no time, but all I could do when the lights went out was laugh out loud.

I think there is no better way to reflect on the deeper meaning of our week on Kilimanjaro and, by extension, life in general. If you can cry when things are wonderful and laugh when they go wrong, you're pretty much on the right track in life.

Perhaps only Africa can teach you this.

EPILOGUE

About a month after our return from Mount Kilimanjaro, I went to a sold-out talk by a guy who jogged along the entire length of India and makes a living giving speeches about his experiences, which are always daring and exhausting and a bit crazy. I was duly impressed by all his adventures until it occurred to me that some of my own adventures have been daring, exhausting, and a bit crazy as well.

That's how the idea to write this book was born. I wanted to share my adventure with a larger audience. I wanted to tell everyone about it: The majesty of snowy Kibo looming over the steppes. The endless walking. The amazing sunrises. The physical strain. The companionship. The laughter. And yes, the toilets (or, rather, their absence).

But most of all I wanted to say that you – yes, you! – should climb Kilimanjaro at least once in your life, if you can somehow find a way, any way at all. It doesn't matter if you're an outdoors kind of person or not. Whether you're terribly fit or not. Or whether you've ever taken a pee in the bushes or not.

If I can climb Mount Kilimanjaro, so can you.

It is an incredible personal journey, both physically and spiritually, and it will forever be a cherished part of your life. You start out with just an idea; a bit of a crazy one perhaps, an idea that gives you a thrill but also fills you with a good dose of dread. You plan and you prepare for months, and when you finally stand at the foot of this mountain that has lived in your thoughts for such a long time, you can't *wait* to get started racing up that slope. And then you walk and you walk, and eventually you start wondering what on Earth possessed you to sign up for such foolishness. Because no matter how far you've come, the summit will remain as elusive as five minutes of peace at our house when all the kids are home. The closer you get, the farther it seems to be out of reach. For days you do nothing but walk uphill, and yet every evening that snow-covered peak seems to hover just as far away as when you started.

You'll vow to never touch drink again, if like me you tend to volunteer for crazy projects after one too many glasses of wine. Or maybe conquering Kilimanjaro has always been on your bucket list, but now that you've had plenty of time to think things through – trust me, while trudging up that mountain you will have more time to think about stuff than you've had in the previous ten years combined – you'll seriously question your sanity. After almost a week of walking, the final stretch to the summit will loom like an insurmountable obstacle, and you'll feel tempted to give up many times when you're creeping up at a snail's pace in the freezing night. If you are fortunate enough to make it all the way up, you realize that you could never have done it on your own but rather needed those around you to carry you up with their collective spirit (or at least to keep you entertained with endless rounds of crude jokes).

What made my Kilimanjaro climb so enjoyable? Certainly, the wonderful people and especially our guides were a huge factor. The fact that I was absolved of kitchen (and Mom) duty for a week was another one. That this was an adventure just for me – even though my son came along – and not for our entire family of six with all their own ideas and opinions on how we should travel. And that we got to witness such natural beauty around us every day, with incredible vistas down the mountain onto the vast African plains below.

Another big factor was, as Adrian later put it, that we slowly detached ourselves from the clutter caused by modern technology. "Maybe we are so busy tweeting and filming and Whatsapping that we don't actually experience the moment anymore," he said to me. "Perhaps the reason for Kilimanjaro being so memorable was because we got down to basics – walking, thinking about our next meal, resting, and maybe listening to some good people singing."

I couldn't have said it any better. Who knew that getting down to basics could be so rewarding?

However, I must warn you: The hardest part of climbing Kilimanjaro might not be the night you scale the summit. It might just be coming home and returning to your prior, rather ordinary life. Just as much as climbing high is inevitably followed by descending low, the emotional high that climbing Kili gives most people is almost always followed by a state of near-depression. I know that I'm not the only one who felt that way.

You find yourself sitting on that airplane home, exhausted and yet unable to sleep for all the emotions swirling around inside of you.

For days afterwards, you wake up in the middle of the night, disoriented and thinking or perhaps wishing you're back in your tent on the mountain.

You sit at your desk for weeks staring into space, not capable of wrapping your head around the ordinary business of daily life, dreaming instead of distant snow-covered peaks and randomly smiling at the memory of a shared joke on the mountain.

You think this can't be it; that your life isn't worth living unless you find another mountain to scale.

You feel closer to fellow Kili climbers, even the ones you've never met, than to your friends and family, and you're surfing the Internet for other people's Kili stories for the temporary relief they provide from your sense of loss.

You replay the Kili song video again and again and have tears in your eyes every time.

It takes time to get through that phase, and it's not always easy. And yet I wouldn't have wanted to miss it for the world. For climbing high and falling low and picking yourself up again to look for the next peak makes your life worth living.

I reflected on all of this as I was listening to India Jogger and his – impressive, I admit – slide show and the life lessons he learned on his journey up and down a subcontinent. And then I thought, why not distill my own life lessons from my journey up and down a mountain into a nicely rounded numbered list? As I've said before, there is nothing like a good list to make you feel as if you've accomplished something of magnitude.

So here I give you, for what they're worth, the 20 lessons Mount Kilimanjaro has taught me:

1. Wherever you are in life, it's always a good idea to plan a new adventure. (But get yourself some good boots and take a few extra packs of wet wipes.)

2. Everyone needs a mountain to scale in their lives. When you're younger, life supplies many a mountain – graduation from high school, going to college, landing a good job, getting married. But during the middle years of your life, things get awfully flat (though often rather bumpy). Climbing a real mountain almost certainly helps put things in perspective.

3. You're much tougher than you think. I'm not trying to glorify anything we did on that mountain, nor do I have any doubts that overall it was still a very pampered experience, summit night notwithstanding,

in comparison to other people's trail adventures. Like the ones where you hike all by yourself, carry the entire staggering load on your own back, run out of water, lose your way, and perhaps encounter a stray bear a la Bill Bryson on his *Walk in the Woods*. But still, climbing gives you confidence that you can deal with anything else that is thrown in your path. Moving forward and overcoming an obstacle often turns out to be the simplest solution, and braving the more difficult path brings immense gratification.

4. Roosevelt was right. The fear of things is worse than the things themselves. I was indeed cold and miserable at five and a half thousand meters, but it wasn't that bad. Or at least it was totally worth it, given the wonderful memories. It's kind of like childbirth: Right afterwards you swear you'll never do it again, but somehow many women end up with more than one child. Maybe certain experiences are only worthwhile when they are as painful as they are uplifting.

5. At the danger of sounding very corny: It's true that it isn't about the destination or the summit, it's about the journey. And who we share it with. Always who we share it with.

6. Whatever it is you take pride in having accomplished, you didn't accomplish it all by yourself. Not ever. There will always be people you couldn't have done it without. And that's okay. In fact, that's the best part.

7. On the other hand, our children *can* eventually do it without us. They will find their own path in life, and when they need help they will come to rely on people other than us, their parents. They will even find someone to carry them off a mountain on their back.

8. A lot of what happens to you is pure chance. Great athletes and the best prepared climbers succumb to altitude sickness on Kili, while people who spend almost no time preparing for it reach the summit just fine. You can't plan your life to the last detail trying to control the outcome, and in any case it won't make you happy. Be open to what happens, don't blame anyone for it, and don't worry about what might have been.

9. And yet, don't leave everything to chance. Whoever remembers to pack enough toilet paper will have the last laugh.

10. There are people who command our respect, no matter what their station in life. I learned more from our guide Godlisten Mkonyi in one week than from some teachers I had for years. Aside from the phrase *Thank you my brother* in Swahili, he taught me to believe in myself and not to worry about what others might think. We spend way too much time worrying about what others might think. A few weeks after our climb, Goddy got to take that trip to South Africa. He stepped on an airplane for the very first time in his life. A surprise party was organized for him in Johannesburg to reunite with previous climbers he had guided, with an overwhelming turnout. And what did he do at the end of the night? He stood up in a restaurant full of strangers and started singing. First one song. Then another. And a third. It brought all our memories rushing back and tears to our eyes. At the end he had the entire waiting staff singing with him, teaching them the Swahili words as doggedly as he had led us up that mountain. Which leads me to the next point:

11. Everyone needs a little singing in their lives.

12. If you can't sing, at least laugh. Everyone needs a lot of laughter in their lives. If you have to make do without a flushable toilet for an entire week to get you to laugh, it's worth it.

13. Dirt and bad smells aren't nearly as terrible as we make them out to be in our sheltered lives. And not looking into a mirror for an entire week is totally liberating.

14. Relax. Pause to look around you or you might miss the beauty. Life is more important than a to-do list. Whatever it is you think you absolutely have to get done today, you can probably still do tomorrow. Especially if today you could rather have coffee with a friend.

15. You are not responsible for someone else's happiness. The only person you can make happy is you. Because it is your own thoughts that control whether you're happy or not. The trick is to discover what brings you happy thoughts. Climbing a mountain is a good start.

16. Consequently, it's okay to do what you want or must do, even if it means doing it alone. I felt guilty wanting to climb Kilimanjaro all for myself, but I've realized that I have a right to want things and do things and become things all on my own, just as much as I cannot begrudge others their right to do the same.

17. You can always take another small step. *Pole pole.* There is almost no limit to what you might accomplish in life if you just go about it *pole pole*, one step at a time. If you're overwhelmed by the task (or mountain) ahead, concentrate on the feet in front of you. Or on the garden trowel, if you must.

18. It's always good to have a change in scenery. If your life seems drab at sea level, maybe you need to take it

to high altitude. At least that's how it worked for us. The higher we climbed, the thinner the air, the more we laughed.

19. Having friends in your life that you can literally walk through shit with is the most valuable gift.

20. Sometimes, it takes a detour over a mountain to find the right path and to know that you're on it. I started out the week signing my name into the logbook at the end of each day with "housewife" as my profession. I ended the week with "writer."

THE END

ACKNOWLEDGEMENTS

There will always be people you couldn't have done it without, and so it is with the writing and production of this book. To all those who've helped make it happen, I would like to express my heartfelt gratitude.

My son Max, without whom I might not have gone to climb Kilimanjaro and would not have had a story to tell.

Godlisten Mkonyi, without whom I might not have gotten back safe and sound from climbing Kilimanjaro, and who inspired me to summon the courage to write this book.

The other wonderful mountain guides – Hillary, Peter, Naiman, and Monday – as well as all the porters, for seeing to our daily comforts, and for doing it with such good humor; hakuna matata!

Dudley, Sharon, Adrian, David, Monia, Martin, and Dylan, for being my companions on this incredible journey, for their support when things got rough, and for the daily dose of laughter; and most of all Mike, the indefatigable, for making it all come together and filling some holes in the story by helping me recall key events.

Klaus, Ben, Maya, and Julia, who stayed behind during my adventure and have since had to make do without cooked meals and folded laundry on many occasions while I've pursued my other love, writing.

My friend Maryanne, for reading all my drafts and for always being there to listen and give encouragement when it was most needed.

Charles O'Donnell, for his helpful tips about the world of self-publishing.

Catherine Ryan Howard, who doesn't know me but whose book "Self-Printed" I read and re-read and consulted every step along the way; it should be on every author's bookshelf.

Maria Foley, for giving so generously of her time as my first proof reader, for pointing out omissions and contradictions, and for her hilarious margin notes.

Tonia, Tricia, and my other new friends in Brentwood, who have so enthusiastically embraced my adventures as an author, for their help in spreading the word of mouth, for their lavish parties and cakes, and for their encouragement.

My editor, Julie van Pelt, not only for finding the glaring inconsistencies in my book and patiently educating me about such things as verb tenses and signposting, but also for giving me faith in my work.

My copy editor, Ros Brodie, for averting many minor and not-so-minor grammatical catastrophes with her nitpicky eye and special wizardry with punctuation and prepositions; I've learned quite a lot about the English language and how to recognize a "jarring" sentence under her guidance.

Nicole El Salamoni, who took a bunch of pictures I sent her, together with "make it funny" and a long succession of new and improved titles, to patiently work her magic and come up with the perfect book cover.

And finally, all my blog readers, too numerous to name, for faithfully following and commenting on my stories over the years; without them, I might not have set out and continued on the road of becoming an author.

BIBLIOGRAPHY

Bezruchka, Stephen, *Altitude Illness: Prevention and Treatment* (Mountaineers Outdoor Expert). Seattle: Mountaineers Books, 2005.

Curtis, Rick, *High Altitude: Acclimatization and Illnesses* (Princeton University Outdoor Action Program). Princeton, 1995.

Dippelreither, Reinhard, *Tansania: Kilimanjaro* (OUTDOOR, Der Weg ist das Ziel). Welver, Germany: Conrad Stein, 2011.

Dorr, Daniel, *Kissing Kilimanjaro: Leaving it All on Top of Africa*. Seattle: Mountaineers Books, 2010.

Meyer, Dr. Hans, *Across East African Glaciers. An Account of the First Ascent of Kilimanjaro*. Translated by E.H.S. Calder. British Library Historical Print Editions, 2011 (George Philip & Son, 1891).

Meyer, Kathleen, *How to Shit in the Woods*. New York: Ten Speed Press, 2011.

Moore, Tim, "Kilimanjaro? Well it nearly killed me." *The Guardian*, 15 Feb 2003.

Stedman, Henry, *Kilimanjaro: The Trekking Guide to Africa's Highest Mountain*. Surrey: Trailblazer Publications, 2010.

Stedman, Henry, "History of Kilimanjaro." www.climbmountkilimanjaro.com, Climb Mount Kilimanjaro, 7 Oct 2006.

Stewart, Alex, *Kilimanjaro: A Complete Trekker's Guide: Preparations, practicalities and trekking routes to the 'Roof of Africa'*. Milnthorpe, UK: Cicerone Press, 2011.

Schoeman, Eben, "Western Breach Route." *Taraji Kilimanjaro*, www.westernbreach.com, 14 Feb 2013.

"Which is the Best Route to Climb Kilimanjaro?" *Team Kilimanjaro*, www.teamkilimanjaro.com, 22 Nov 2010.

"Which Route Should I Use to Climb Kilimanjaro?" *Ultimate Kilimanjaro*, www.ultimatekilimanjaro.com, 25 Oct 2009.

Wikipedia contributors, "Mount Kilimanjaro." *Wikipedia, The Free Encyclopedia*. en.wikipedia.org, 14 Feb 2014

What to Pack for Kilimanjaro?

It is a topic that will cause the prospective Kili climber no small amount of anxiety, starting from the day the trip is booked until departure. Having a ready packing list, battle-tested by a veteran, can make all the difference for a successful climb.

To see a comprehensive packing list and tips on routes and climbing seasons, as well as a full gallery of color photographs from the Kilimanjaro adventure recounted in this book, visit the author's website:

www.evamelusinethieme.com

Finally, if you enjoyed *Kilimanjaro Diaries*, please take a few minutes to leave a review on **www.amazon.com** or **www.goodreads.com**.

ABOUT THE AUTHOR

Eva Melusine Thieme is the author of the popular blog *Joburg Expat*, where she has been chronicling her family's African adventures while living in Johannesburg. Before that, she was a freelance writer for *Kansas City Parent Magazine*. She was born in Germany and has lived in North America, Asia, and Africa. She currently resides in Brentwood, Tennessee, with her husband and four children, where she is working on her next book about a road trip through Namibia with six people in a five-person car.

Made in the USA
Lexington, KY
22 January 2018